CW00692427

An Introduction To Comparative Anatomy And Physiology : Being The Two Introductory Lectures Delivered At The Royal College Of Surgeons, On The 21st And 25th Of March, 1816

Lawrence, William, Sir, 1783-1867

AN

INTRODUCTION

TO

𝔈𝔬𝔪𝔭𝔞𝔯𝔞𝔱𝔦𝔳𝔢 𝔄𝔫𝔞𝔱𝔬𝔪𝔶

AND

PHYSIOLOGY;

BEING THE

TWO INTRODUCTORY LECTURES

DELIVERED AT THE

ROYAL COLLEGE OF SURGEONS,

On the 21st and 25th of March, 1816.

═══════

BY

WILLIAM LAWRENCE, F. R. S.

PROFESSOR OF ANATOMY AND SURGERY TO THE COLLEGE; ASSISTANT SURGEON TO ST
BARTHOLOMEW'S HOSPITAL; SURGEON TO BETHLEHEM AND BRIDEWELL HOSPITALS,
AND TO THE LONDON INFIRMARY FOR DISEASES OF THE EYE.

═══════

LONDON:

PRINTED FOR J CALLOW, MEDICAL BOOKSELLER,
No. 10, CROWN COURT, PRINCES STREET, SOHO

1816.

BARNARD AND FARLEY,
Skinner-Street, London.

Dedication.

AS a Testimony of sincere Esteem for a Character adorned by the greatest Urbanity and Benevolence, and dignified by the nicest Sense of Honour, and the most exalted Principles;

And of the highest Respect for distinguished Talents, assiduously and successfully employed in advancing a Science, and practising

A 2

a Profession most useful to Mankind;

THE FOLLOWING PAGES ARE

INSCRIBED

TO

J. R. FARRE, M. D.

PHYSICIAN TO THE LONDON INFIRMARY FOR DISEASES OF
THE EYE,

BY HIS

FRIEND AND COLLEAGUE,

THE AUTHOR.

ADVERTISEMENT.

THE following Lectures, not composed
with any view to their Publication, are
now printed in consequence of the Author
having been repeatedly asked for Copies
of them. The Notes and References,
which obviously could not have formed
any part of the Lectures as delivered,
have been added from a notion that they
may be found useful by Students.

In several parts of the Second Lecture
the Views correspond with those which
have been entertained and published on

the same Subjects by Cuvier and Bichat; whose Words are occasionally employed with slight Alterations. Having been compelled to do this in the first instance by want of Time, the Author has preferred leaving these Passages with the present general Acknowledgment, to exchanging them for original ones, because he wished to print the Lectures exactly as they were delivered; not having occasion to alter any of the Statements, which are the result of such Reflection and Judgment, as he could employ on the Subjects.

College of Physicians,
    July, 1816.

CONTENTS.

LECTURE I.

INTRODUCTION,

&c. &c.

LECTURE I.

OBJECTS AND HISTORY OF COMPARATIVE ANATOMY.

GENTLEMEN,

BEFORE I enter on the subject of this Lecture, I shall request your attention, for a few minutes, to the circumstances under which I appear before you on the present occasion :—on such a subject I shall detain you as shortly as possible.

It was not till the latter part of last summer, that the Court of Assistants of this College did me the honour of appointing me one of their Professors: an appointment, which I freely acknowledge to have been most gratifying to my feelings, not only on account of the body who conferred it, but when I considered to whom I had succeeded,* and to whom I became associated.† To your feelings I must trust for an excuse, if any be thought necessary, for taking this earliest opportunity of giving utterance to the sentiments of respect and gratitude I entertain for the latter gentleman. You and the public know, and have long known his acute mind, his peculiar talent for observation, his zeal for the advancement of surgery, and his successful exertions in improving the scientific knowledge and treatment of disease. · His singular happiness in developing and teaching to others the original, and philosophic views, which he naturally takes of all the subjects that come under his examination; and the success, with which he communi-

---

* Astley Cooper, Esq.   † J. Abernethy, Esq.

cates that enthusiasm in the cause of science and humanity, which is so warmly felt by himself; the admirable skill, with which he enlivens the dry details of elementary instruction; are most gratefully acknowledged by his numerous pupils. All these various excellencies have been repeatedly felt in this Theatre. Having had the good fortune to be initiated in the profession by Mr. Abernethy, and to have lived for many years under his roof, I can assure you, with the greatest sincerity, that however highly the public may estimate the surgeon and the philosopher, I have reason to speak still more highly of the Man and the Friend; of the invariable kindness, which directed my early studies and pursuits, of the disinterested friendship, which has assisted every step of my progress in life, of the benevolent and honourable feelings, the independent spirit, and the liberal conduct, which, while they dignify our profession, win our love and command our respect for genius and knowledge, converting these precious gifts into instruments of the most extensive public good.

Since the choice of the College was announced to me, my time has been so occupied, partly by engagements previously formed, and partly by others, not then foreseen, that it was not possible for me to make any preparations for the course before the period* when it was opened by Mr. Abernethy.   How small a part of the ·time, which has since elapsed, can have been spared from public and private professional occupations, you will easily understand ; and you will, I am sure, make every allowance for the imperfections of that labour, which has been entirely prosecuted in the evening and

---

* The 25th of Januaiy.

night after the exertions and fatigues of the day.   By deferring these lectures till next spring, I should have consulted my own ease, and might perhaps have hoped to render them less unworthy of the subject and the audience.   But I was averse to interrupt the arrangements of the College, or to disappoint its members, in their expectation of an annual course of comparative anatomy.   However strange it may sound, the very magnitude of the subject, and the consciousness of my inability to do it justice, were further motives for proceeding without delay.— The short and uncertain intervals of leisure afforded by a professional life could not supply the numerous and important deficiencies of which I am conscious ; and the expectation that would naturally arise from delay could not be satisfied by the performance.   In offering to you therefore such information on comparative anatomy, as I acquired some years ago, in a cursory attention to it, principally as a source of amusement, I must throw myself entirely on your indulgence. This I should have found it necessary to appeal to, even under the most favourable circumstances of time and opportunities, when I appear before you in the chair successively occupied by Sir Everard Home and Mr. Cooper. I must entreat you to forget the talents, the performances, and the reputation of these gentlemen; and to make in my behalf all the allowance that is due to disparity of age, want of opportunity, and deficient preparation.

With this explanation, then, I undertake the task confided to me by the court; availing myself of the occasion to assure its members that I value the appointment most highly, as an unsolicited proof of their good opinion. I feel grateful to them on public grounds for the pains they have taken to improve surgical education, and consequently to increase the respectability of surgeons. By preparing a suitable building for the magnificent and invaluable collection formed by an English surgeon, by providing for its preservation and increase, and establishing lectures for its illustration, they have finally rescued surgery from the state, in which it was too long kept, of a mechanical and subordinate department of the healing art, and have elevated it to its proper rank of an independent science. While the seniors of our profession are thus laudably engaged in endeavouring to raise it in public estimation by rendering it more worthy of public confidence, it is particularly incumbent on the younger members to co-operate in the same plans. This consideration would always be a motive with me for undertaking any public duty, in which I could lend assistance, however feeble, in supporting the character and rank of surgery.

The anatomy of animals having been investigated at first, in order to throw light on the organization and functions of the human body, the expression comparative anatomy was employed to designate the structure of animals, compared to that of man, as a standard. It is now used in a more extensive sense, and means the anatomy of all living beings compared to each other. It thus furnishes the data, which constitute the basis of general physiology, of which the object is to determine the laws, that regulate the phenomena exhibited by organized beings. Comparative anatomy bears the same relation to general physiology, that human anatomy does to human physiology; the latter expression denoting the science which is employed in ascertaining the vital phenomena of man.

Natural History, or, to use the most comprehensive term, *Zoology*, is not opposed to comparative anatomy, but includes it; the structure of an animal forming part, and a most important, though too often neglected part, of its history.

Our first step in the study of life is to examine the organs, that are its material instruments; and to ascertain their visible structure: but this examination must not be confined to one animal. We should endeavour to discover what is the essential circumstance, the necessary condition to the occurrence of the phenomena. The organs must therefore be viewed under all their modifications of greater and less simplicity, of combination with others, &c.; they must be surveyed in every kind of

animal: and such labours only can lead
to any satisfactory knowledge of general
structure.   The phenomena of life must
be studied in the same way; the functions
must be observed and compared in all the
links of the great chain of beings, to whom
any modification of vitality has been im-
parted.

It is the series of such facts that com-
poses hitherto the science of physiology;
it is only by comparing these that we can
hope to ascend to general causes, and to
deduce common laws.

The connexion and mutual influences of
the various organs oppose great and insu-
perable obstacles to our knowledge of the
precise effect and importance of each.
Here comparative anatomy comes to our
aid: we find, in the various classes of
animals, almost every possible combina-

tion of organs, and there is no organ, which is not wanting in some class or other. The effect of such combinations and privations cannot but illustrate the nature and operations of the part in question. Fishes have no tympanum, nor external ear; insects no circulating system, many of the lower orders no brain nor nervous system.

In viewing the subject of life, we should be led to the most erroneous conclusions, if we confined our survey to man, or to the more complicated animals nearly allied to him. The only way to avoid such errors, and to rectify our notions, is to extend our views over the whole animated creation. A slight injury of the brain will destroy a man or a mammiferous quadruped; a smart blow on the skull, or the effusion of a little blood are sufficient; while the removal of the whole cranial contents is by no means suddenly fatal in the frog, turtle, and other reptiles.

" In the beginning of November, Redi opened the skull of a land tortoise, and removed the whole brain. The tortoise did not seem to suffer; it moved about as before; but groping its way; for the eyes soon shut after losing the brain, and never opened again. A fleshy integument formed, which covered the opening of the skull; and in this state the animal lived until May, that is six complete months. Spallanzani deprived four frogs of the brain: two lived till the fifth day. He also deprived three newts of the brain: they suffered violent convulsions; their eyes closed; they hardly moved from one place to another; and expired about the middle of the third day. He cut out the heart of three newts: they took to flight, leapt, swam, and executed the same functions as before; however, all died in forty-eight hours. Four frogs, deprived of the heart, kept their eyes open, and preserved the use of their limbs. They survived thirty-six hours."*

What a contrast is there between the precarious tenure of life in man and the higher orders of animals, where the various organs are connected by numerous sympathies, and where the whole system is influenced by the affections of each part, so that disorders and destruction are constantly impending; and the simple but powerful vitality of the hair-worm (gordius), or the wheel animal (vorticella rotatoria), which after remaining for years in

---

* Spallanzani's Tracts on the Nature of Animals and Vegetables; v. 1. Introductory Observations, p. 45.

a dried state resume life and motion on being moistened. *

The power of reproduction—of restoring or renewing parts, that have been mutilated or entirely lost, is one of the most striking characters of organized bodies. It is one of the most important provisions of nature, inasmuch as it guards animals and plants against the multiplied dangers to which their bodies are exposed. Hence, when viewed in connexion with the system of nutrition altogether, it forms one of those decisive and grand characters, which distinguish at once the machines, that proceed from the hand of the Creator, from all, even the most ingenious and boasted productions

* Leeuwenhoeck Epist. ad Societatem regiam, aliosque illustres viros; Leid. 1719, 4to. and Arcana Natura continuata; 4to. Baker's Employment for the Microscope, 1764. Spallanzani's Tracts, v. 2. tr. 4.

of human skill. The difference is recognised at the first glance: the distance is
immeasurable.   The springs and wheels
of mechanical instruments have no power
of repairing themselves, when they are
bent, broken, worn, or spoiled; but such a
faculty is enjoyed in various degrees by
every animal, and by every plant.   It
exists, however, in very different degrees in
the different departments of the animal
kingdom.   In man, and such animals as
are nearly allied to him, it is very limited,
although sufficiently active to be capable
of remedying the effects of great injuries.
If a bone be broken, a muscle or tendon
divided, or a piece of skin destroyed, processes are set up in the parts, by which
restoration is accomplished.   The ends of
the bone are joined by an osseous substance, which gives to the part its original
solidity, the tendon regains its firmness

and power of resistance; the muscle will contract again, and move the points of its attachment; and the surface of the body is covered by a new piece of integument. In the cases, which have been just mentioned, the restorative power repairs injuries, but it goes no further: neither in man, nor in any warm-blooded animals are entire organs ever reproduced. If a limb be cut off, or a piece of flesh taken away, the wound is healed, the sides of the chasm grow together; but the lost parts are never formed again. In the lower orders of the animal kingdom, on the contrary, such are the strength and perfection of the reproductive energy, that considerable members are restored, and we can hardly assign a limit to the power in some instances. The lower we descend in the scale of beings, the more surprising are the manifestations of this reproductive faculty.

The large claws of the crab and lobster, and the entire limbs or tail of the newt* can be restored : the same holds good of the rays of the star-fish and the arms or tentacula of the cuttle-fish. The entire eye of the water newt, with all its coats

---

* There is an interesting account in the Memoires de l'Acad. des Sciences de Paris, 1686, particularly of the restoration of the tail of lizards. Spallanzani, Bonnet, and Blumenbach, have employed themselves in researches on this subject. The former first called the attention of the public to it in his " Prodromo di un opera da imprimersi sopra le riproduzione animali." Bonnet published his memoir on the reproduction of the limbs of the water newt in the Journal de Physique, 1777. His Enquiries were again published in his Œuvres d'Histoire Naturelle, t. 5; and there are three memoirs by him on the subject, translated into English, in Spallanzani's Tracts on the Natural History of Animals and Vegetables, v. 2. The experiments of Blumenbach are contained in his " Specimen Physiologiæ Comparatæ inter animalia calidi et frigidi Sanguinis." 4to.

and humours has been extirpated, and in
the course of ten months succeeded by a
new and perfect eye-ball.* The whole
head of the common snail, with its four

---

* " With a scalpel," says Bonnet, " I extracted the
right eye of a large newt on the 13th of September,
1779, but I did not obtain the globe without much
injury to the tunics. A deep bloody wound in the
socket of the eye was the consequence of this cruel
operation; and the reader will not be surprised if I
hardly expected any thing from it, and that the newt
would probably remain blind for ever. How great was
my astonishment, therefore, when on the 31st of May,
1780, I saw a new eye formed by nature. The iris
and cornea were already well shaped; but the latter
wanted its peculiar transparency, which is very considerable in these animals. The restoration was complete on the 1st of September.; the cornea being
transparent, and the iris having acquired its yellow
gilded colour. On the 8th of November, 1780, it
differed from the other eye only in being a little
smaller, and in the iris or golden circle going only
half round the ball." Spallanzani's Tracts, &c. v. 2,
p. 432, et seq.

horns has been reproduced, after being removed in experiments, in many in-

---

"I repeated," says Blumenbach, "the experiment of the celebrated Bonnet concerning the reproduction of the eye in the water newt. I cut out the whole globe, at the insertion of the optic nerve, in three instances, in neither of which was the organ reproduced: but a white and firm fungus, shooting from the cut end of the nerve, gradually filled the orbit, the animals themselves becoming affected with a kind of dropsical swelling, and dying in a few months. Instructed by these failures, I proceeded to operate in a different way on a fourth animal, in May, 1784. I first divided the cornea, to let out the lens and other humours, and then cut away the remaining empty and collapsed coats, leaving a small portion of the common coverings of the bulb, which, from a careful examination with a glass in water of the parts removed, I judge to have been scarcely equal to one-fifth of the whole globe. In the following months the whole orbit seemed to be filled by the approximated eyelids, which, however, began to separate in the sixth month after the operation, and thus disclosed a new little bulb springing up from the bottom of the orbit. This new globe was still much smaller than the other in

stances.*   If the earth-worm† or actinia‡
(the sea ancmonc) be cut in two, each half
will become a perfect animal.   The fresh
water polype may even be cut into several
pieces: each of which will become a perfect polype.

The extensive examination of various
structures is not only a necessary ground-
work for the edifice of general physiology,
but it has thrown great light on the orga-

April, 1785, when the animal died accidentally, though
in other respects it was most perfect, exhibiting the
golden iris, with its regular pupillar aperture behind
the cornea; all which points are clearly distinguish-
able in the preparation, which I preserved." Specimen,
p. 31.

* Spallanzani's Tracts, v. 2.

† Reaumur Mem. pour servir à l'Hist. Nat. des Insectes: t. 6. Preface.

Spallanzani, prodromo di un opera sopra le riproduzione animali.

‡ An essay towards elucidating the history of the
Sea-anemones, by Abbé Dicquemare. Philos. Trans.
vol. 63.

nization and functions of the human frame. " Quotidie experior," says Haller,* " de plerarumque partium corporis animati functione non posse sincerum judicium ferri, nisi ejusdem partis fabrica et in homine, et in variis quadrupedibus, et in avibus, et in piscibus, sæpe etiam et in insectis innotuerit." Whoever will reflect on our present knowledge of the digestive, respiratory, generative, or other processes of man, and will review the successive stages of its progress, will find that comparative anatomy has rendered us the most essential assistance, and will be disposed to agree with Haller, when he asserts that physiology has been more illustrated by the dissection of animals than by that of the human subject. The formation of the germ in the ovary, and its passage through the Fallopian tube into the uterus, could not have

* Elementa Physiologiæ. Pref.

been discovered in man. Although they are now universally believed, they rest, not on actual demonstration, but on analogy and other indirect arguments. In birds, fishes, and reptiles, these points admit of the clearest and most direct proof.

Doubts were entertained respecting the functions and relative importance of the two organs composing the human biliary system; whether the bile were formed in the liver, or in the gall bladder, or in both. These points could hardly be determined from the human body only; but we look at animals. We find in many large quadrupeds that bile is secreted in the liver alone, without any gall bladder; that no animal has the latter without the former part; that in all which have a gall bladder this receptacle is either attached to the liver, or communicates with its secretory duct. We conclude, therefore, that the liver is essential to the formation of bile; that the gall bladder is not essential; and that this fluid passes from the liver in which it is formed, into the gall bladder.

Comparative anatomy is again of the greatest importance in reference to natural history. There is a close correspondence between the structure and the habits of animals, and they mutually illustrate each other. The quadruped, which has to pursue and to kill his prey, has instruments of motion altogether different from those of the animals who collect their food from the vegetable kingdom. The jaws, the teeth, and all the digestive apparatus are equally different in the two cases. The creatures which burrow under ground, are very differently constructed from those which live in trees, or such as inhabit the water. In short the organization is universally in relation to the mode of life;

and, in consequence of their reciprocal influence, all the various parts of an animal are so closely connected to each other, that this relation may be traced even in the minutest particulars.* The succeeding Lectures will be a continued illustration

---

* The mutual relations of the organs, and the laws of co-existence, to which their combinations are subjected, are so well pointed out by Cuvier, that I quote his words, as the work in which they occur, is not so generally known in this country, as the other productions of this justly celebrated zoologist.

" Every organized being consists of parts, which correspond mutually, which concur by means of reciprocal influences in the production of a common end, and thus form together a whole, a perfect system. No one part can change, without the others being modified; and consequently each, taken separately, indicates all the others.

" Thus, if the intestines of an animal are adapted by their organization to digest flesh, and that in a

of this point.   No branch of natural knowledge is more interesting than a contem-

---

recent state, the jaws must be constructed for devour-
ing prey; the claws for seizing and tearing it; the
teeth for lacerating and dividing its flesh; the whole
apparatus of moving powers for pursuing and over-
taking it; the organs of sense for perceiving it at a
distance;—nature must moreover implant in the brain
an impulse or instinct, leading such a creature to con-
ceal itself and lay in wait for its victims. Such are
the general conditions of the carnivorous regimen:
every flesh-devouring animal unites them necessarily;
for its species could not otherwise subsist. But, besides these general conditions, there are subordinate
ones, relating to the size, the species, and the abode
of the prey; and each of these secondary conditions
gives rise to differences of detail in the forms which
result from the general laws. Hence, not only the
class, but the order, the genus, and even the species
are expressed in the form of each part.

" To give the jaw the power of seizing, a particular
form of condyle is necessary; there must be a certain
relation between the position of the resistance, the

plation of the infinitely diversified organic arrangements, by which animals are adapt-

---

moving power and the fulcrum; a certain volume in the temporal muscle, requiring a proportional capacity in the fossa which lodges it; and a proportionate convexity in the Zygomatic arch, under which it passes; this bony arch must also possess a certain strength, to support the action of the masseter.

" In bearing away the prey, a certain force is required in the muscles that raise the head; hence the necessity of a determinate form in the vertebræ, whence these muscles arise, and in the occiput, where they are inserted.

" For dividing flesh, cutting teeth are required; and they must be more or less cutting, in proportion as they are more or less exclusively occupied in that way. Their basis must be solid, if they are employed in breaking and comminuting bones, particularly if the bones are strong. These circumstances will influence the development of all the parts employed in moving the jaw.

ed to their respective places in the creation. In this way the researches of comparative

---

" Mobility of the toes, and strength of the nails are necessary for seizing the prey; hence arise determinate forms of the phalanges and particular distributions of muscles and tendons.   There must be a power of rotating the fore-arm, and consequently a particular form of the bones composing it : and as the latter are articulated to the humerus, any alterations in them must modify its figure.   Animals, which employ their fore-limbs in seizing, must have strong shoulders; the scapulæ and clavicles will therefore exhibit certain modifications.   The muscles must have forms, size, and strength suitable to the actions, of which the bones and joints just enumerated are capable; while their attachments and contractions impress particular figures on those solid organs.

" Similar conclusions may be drawn respecting the posterior extremities, which contribute to the rapidity of the general motions; respecting the composition of the trunk, and the form of the vertebræ, which influence the facility of those motions; respecting the bones of the nose, of the orbit, and the ear, which have

anatomy furnish the only data, on which
we can proceed with security in the clas-

---

obvious relations to the degree of perfection in the
senses of smelling, seeing, and hearing. In a word,
the form of the tooth determines that of the condyle;
the form of the scapula that of the nails; just as the
equation of a curve indicates all its properties. As in
taking each property separately for the basis of a particular equation, we might arrive, not only at the
ordinary equation, but at all the other properties
whatever; so the nail, the scapula, the maxillary
condyle, the femur, and all the other bones taken separately, would each indicate the kind of teeth, or
would indicate each other reciprocally; and, beginning
with either separately, we might, according to the rational laws of the organic economy, construct the whole
animal."

Recherches sur les ossemens fossiles de quadrupèdes;
discours preliminaire, p. 58, et suiv. The whole of
this very scientific and valuable work is a successful
and happy illustration of the principles just explained.

sific arrangements of natural history; and
they lead always to that natural arrangement of animals, which should be the chief
object of all classification.

The comparative anatomist discovers
that the whale tribe, although inhabiting
the ocean, agree in all the essential points of
their structure with mammiferous quadrupeds, and therefore are not, properly speaking, fishes.   In the crab and lobster, and in
the inhabitants of the various marine shells,
he finds beings of the most different organization and habits, although confounded
under the common name of shell-fish, and
he finds both of these kinds of animals
altogether different in structure from
fishes.

Such being the importance of comparative anatomy, to the physiologist, who

draws from it the facts, on which his knowledge of the functions of animals is grounded; to the natural historian, who finds in it a clue to guide his steps through what appears at first the inextricable labyrinth of animated nature; to the physician and surgeon, whose pathological reasonings can only be relied on, when built on the broad foundation of general physiology; and to the natural theologian, who discovers in the modifications of structure, according to situation and circumstances, and its constant relation to the wants, habits, and powers of animals, the strongest evidence of final purposes, and therefore the strongest proof of an intelligent first cause; we shall not wonder that this subject has powerfully attracted attention at all times, and has been prosecuted by some of the most considerable geniuses.

The first* of these is Aristotle, who is not only the oldest author on comparative anatomy, whose writings we possess, but one of those who have displayed the greatest genius in this branch of natural history, and who offers the best model for such researches. His renown as a philosopher, who exercised unlimited and undisputed sway over the minds of men for two thousand years, and the just celebrity of his writings on logic, criticism, ethics,

---

* Democritus of Abdera is said to have devoted much of his time to the dissection of animals, and to have investigated, among other subjects, the source and passages of the bile, and the cause of madness. But neither he, nor the famous Alexandrian anatomists, Herophilus and Erasistratus, who were rather posterior to Aristotle, and who had noticed the lacteal vessels in animals, left behind them any account of their labours, which we therefore are only acquainted with from their being incidentally mentioned by other writers.

politics, have been unfavorable to his reputation as a natural historian, although
his work on the history of animals, περι
ζωων ίσορίας,* (which too is only an abridg-
ment of the original production), has not
been equalled, even to the present day, in
the magnitude of the field which it embraces; and the number, variety, and extent of the original observations which it
contains. The noble patronage of his
pupil Alexander enabled the philosopher
to expend an enormous sum in drawing
together from all quarters the animals de-

---

* Aristotelis historia animalium, Græce et Latine,
cum versione et commentariis J. C. Scaligeri, Tolosæ,
1619, fol. I believe it has been lately republished in
Germany, with valuable notes and illustrations by
Schneider. There is a French translation by Camus,
who unfortunately was not so well versed, as could
have been wished, either in the knowledge of Greek,
or of natural history. Histoire des Animaux d'Aristote,
avec le texte en regard, 2 tom. 4to. Paris, 1783.

scribed in this immortal work. He not only knew and dissected a great number of species, but he studied and described them on a vast and luminous plan, to which none of his successors has approached, ranging the facts, not according to the species, but to the organs and functions—the only means of arriving at comparative results. - The modern works of Blumenbach and Cuvier, are constructed on the same principle, which was also followed by Mr. Hunter in the arrangement of his collection.

The chief divisions, which naturalists follow at present in the animal kingdom, were established by Aristotle; and he has indicated several, to which modern naturalists have recurred, after they had been long unwisely neglected. His great distribution of animals into those which have blood, and those which have not, (the former including mammalia, birds, reptiles, and fishes; the latter the mollusca, crustacea, testacea, and insects), is the same with that proposed by the French naturalists, and now universally adopted, although the ground of the division, the presence or absence of blood is not correct. Lamarck has drawn his character, and his name for these two primary divisions from the possession or want of the vertebral column.

The four classes of insects, mollusca, crustacea, and testacea, which constitute his second division, are a much more natural and philosophic distribution than that of Linneus, by whom they are crowded together into the two classes of Insects and Vermes.

In many details he is more correct than those who have followed him. For example, he states that the crocodile moves the upper jaw; which, after being long represented as a vulgar error, is now found to be true by the report of the naturalists who accompanied the French expedition to Egypt. It is allowed by a very competent judge (Cuvier), that Aristotle's account of the elephant is more accurate than that of Buffon.

It is to be regretted that the Romans had not an Aristotle, as facilities existed, while that wonderful people held the reins of empire, for studying some parts of zoology, which have not occurred again. The largest and rarest animals brought from all parts of the empire, were exhibited in the triumphs, the public games, and the theatres, to amuse the inhabitants of the imperial city. They saw the hippopotamus, the two horned rhinoceros, and the camelopard, which have not been brought alive into

Europe since. Commodus exhibited five
hippopotami at one time, and ten came-
lopards were shewn by Gordian III. Other
foreign and remarkable animals were quite
common, as the. lion, elephant, panther,
&c. Augustus shewed twenty-five living
crocodiles at once.*

Galen dissected animals and performed
numerous experiments on them, some of
which are of a nice and rather difficult
kind, as tying or dividing nerves, &c. His
anatomical descriptions are obviously
drawn from these sources, particularly from
the monkey tribe;† to which he would
naturally be led by their acknowledged.

* See Cuvier sur les Ossemens Fossiles; Discours
preliminaire, and the chapters on the Osteology of the
Rhinoceros and Hippopotamus.

† This point is clearly established by Vesalius, in
his Epistola de radicis Chinæ usu; and it is still more

relationship to our species. It is doubtful whether he ever dissected the human body. As a comparative anatomist, however, Galen hardly deserves mention; and certainly not in conjunction with Aristotle, whose admirable work is followed by a long and barren interval of many centuries, in which this branch of natural knowledge like all others, was not merely stationary, but lamentably retrograde.

Among the restorers of anatomy, at the revival of learning in the sixteenth century, and particularly in the Italian school, to which in this period we are almost entirely indebted for encouraging these pursuits, and diffusing a taste for them

satisfactorily proved by Camper; see his Remarks " sur l'Orang-utang, et quelques autres Especes de singes;" Introduction, § 5. et suiv. in the Œuvres d'Histoire Naturelle, &c. t. 1.

over the rest of Europe, there were some
who cultivated the anatomy of animals,
and who have recorded the results of their
labours.   In his Natural History of Birds,
Belon* has devoted a book to their anatomy, and Rondelet, professor in the university of Montpellier, illustrated the history
of fishes, and other marine animals in a
very valuable work,† which abounds with
instructive details in comparative anatomy.
Coiter, of Groningen, who had studied
under Fallopius, Rondelet and Aldrobandi,
published some excellent plates on comparative Osteology.‡   Ruini, a senator of

---

* L'histoire de la nature des oiseaux, avec leur
descriptions et naiſs Portraits; en six livres. 1555.

† De Piscibus marinis libri xviii; Lugdun. 1554.

Pars altera, in qua pisces aquæ dulcis, ranæ, tes-
tudines, lacertæ et amphibia aliqua continentur; 1555.

‡ Diversorum animalium sceletorum explicationes,

Bologna, described the anatomy of the horse in a large work with plates.* Fabricius, professor at Padua, and the instructor of Harvey, devoted a splendid volume† to the formation of the fœtus, and among other subjects, explained the mechanism of animal motions.‡ His disciple, Casserius investigated the structure of the larynx, and of the organs of sense.§ But

---

cum lectionibus. Gab. Fallopii de partibus similaribus humani corporis. Norimb. 1575.

There are also many observations relating to comparative anatomy in his larger work; Externarum et internarum humani corporis partium tabulæ, &c. 1573.

* Anatomia del Cavallo, infirmità, e suoi remedii. Bologna, 1598. 4to.

† De formato fœtu, Patavii, 1600. Fol.

‡ De motu animalium secundum totum, Patav. 1618, 4to.

§ De vocis auditusque organis, Ferrar. 1600. Fol.

Aldrobandi of Bologna, or in his Latin name, by which he is better known,. Aldrovandus, deserves the first rank in these times for his labours in the whole circle of Zoology. He established a collection of all objects that could illustrate his favourite pursuits, and paid considerable attention to the structure of animals. Of the numerous folios, which bear his. name, the three* which are devoted to ornithology (the history of birds) are all that were published in his own life; and they are the most valuable with reference to comparative anatomy.

In the first half of the seventeenth

Pentæstheseion, h. e. de quinque sensibus liber, Venet.,1609, fol.

* Ornithologiæ, seu de avibus historiæ libri. Bonon. Fol. 1599—1603.

century, when schools of anatomy were not yet established, and great part of Europe, particularly Germany, was desolated ·by civil war, anatomical inquirers turned their attention to animals : comparative anatomy was now cultivated with considerable ardour in most countries of Europe, and numerous experiments were made on living animals. If the human subject was at this time too much neglected, a neglect caused more by the want of opportunities than of zeal, many great discoveries were ·made in animals, that illustrated equally the human structure and functions, and ultimately revolutionized the whole fabric of physiology and pathology. The discovery of the circulation*

---

* Exercitatio anatomica de motu cordis et sanguinis in animalibus; Francf. 1628, 4to.

and of the process of generation * by
Harvey, of the lacteals by Aselli,† of the
thoracic duct by Pecquet,‡ and of the
lymphatics by Rudbek§ or Bartholin,‖ are

---

* Exercitationes de generatione animalium, quibus
accedunt quædam de partu, de membranis et humo-
ribus, de conceptione, &c. Lond. 1651, 4to.

† Dissertatio de lacteis venis, quarto vasorum mesa-
raicorum genere, novo invento, &c. Mediolani, 1627.
4to.

‡ Experimenta nova anatomica, quibus incognitum
chyli receptaculum, et ab eo per thoracem in ramos
usque subclavios vasa lactea deteguntur. Paris, 1651,
4to.

§ Diss. de Circulatione Sanguinis, Arosiæ, 1652,
4to. Nova Exercitatio Anatomica, exhibens ductus
hepatis aquosos, et vasa glandularum serosa, 1653,
4to. Published also in Haller's Disp. Anat. select.
See also Haller, Bibliotheca Anatomica, t. I. § 415.

‖ Diss. de Lacteis Thoracicis in homine Brutisque
nuperrime Observatis; Hafniæ, 1652.

some of the results for which we are indebted to the researches of that time in comparative anatomy.

Many other valuable contributions to our knowledge of the structure and functions of animals were made about the same time, and were most signally aided by the two inventions of the microscope and anatomical injections, which opened a new world to the cultivators of anatomy and natural history. These powerful instruments of research were very successfully employed by Malpighi and Swammerdam. The former described the silk-worm with great minuteness and fidelity, leaving very

---

Vasa lymphatica nuper in animantibus inventa, et hepatis Exsequiæ; Hafn. 1653.

Vasa lymphatica in homine nuper inventa; 1654.

Haller's Bibliotheca Anatomica, t. 1. § 378.

little for future observers.;* Swammerdam
executed his researches on the structure
and habits of insects, a wonderful monu-
ment of patient industry.† Leeuwen-

---

* Dissertatio Epistolica de Bombyce, Londin. 1669,
4to.

† Historia generalis insectorum, Leid. '1685', 4to.
This is a translation from the original Dutch; Alge-
meene Verhandeling van de Bloedeloose diertjens;
Utrecht, 1669.

But for the work, which will immortalize the name
of Swammerdam, we are partly indebted to the libe-
rality and love of science of Boerhaave, who purchased
the manuscripts and drawings, which the author had
been compelled by poverty to part with before his
death, and had them published in the Dutch and Latin
languages, under the title Biblia Naturæ, seu Historia
insectorum in certas Classes reducta, nec non Ex-
emplis et Anatomico variorum animalculorum examine
illustrata, &c.   Leid. 1737, fol.   This includes the
former work.

hoeck,* Hooke,† and Baker‡ employed themselves very assiduously in microscopic researches, some of which relate to the structure of the more minute classes of living beings. Redi, whose works are allowed by his countrymen to be excellent models of pure Italian style, dissipated the prevailing errors and prejudices concerning the generation of insects, and illustrated many parts of physiology and comparative anatomy by dissections, experiments, and observations.§ His pupil, Lorenzini, published an excellent anatomy

---

* Opera omnia, Leid. 1722, 4to. 4 v.

† Micrographia, Lond. fol. 1665, and numerous papers in the early volumes of the Philosophical Transactions.

‡ Microscope made easy, Lond. 1743. 8vo.
Employment for the Microscope, 1753.

§ Osservazioni intorno alle vipere, Firenze, 1664.
Esperienze intorno alla generazione degl'insetti, 1668.

of the torpedo. * Valisnieri employed himself successfully in the investigation of insects, and on other subjects.† Our countryman Tyson has described several animals with great accuracy, as the rattle-snake,‡ the Tajassu,§ the opossum,‖ the porpoise,¶ and the orang utang.   His ac-

---

Esperienze intorno a diverse cose Naturali, &c. 1671.

Osservazioni intorno agli Animali viventi negli altri Animali viventi, 1684.

His works were all published together, Naples, 1687, 8vo. or in a more complete collection, 1728, 4to.

* Osservazioni intorno alle torpedini; Firenze, 1678, 4to.

† Opere Fisico-Mathematiche, Venez. 3 t. fol. 1733.

‡ Philosophical Transactions, No. 144.

§ Ibid. No. 153.

‖ Carigueya, seu Marsupiale Americanum, or the anatomy of an opossum dissected at Gresham College; Lond. 1698, 4to. and in the Philosophical Transactions, No. 239.

¶ Phocœna, or the anatomy of a porpess; 1680, 4to.

count of the latter under the title of Anatomy of the Pigmy,* although encum-
bered with much useless learning, is as
perfect and satisfactory an anatomical
history as we possess of any animal to
the present time. The same observation
is equally applicable to the anatomy of
the turtle and tortoise published at Florence by Caldesi. †   Lister paid great attention to the anatomy of the mollusca,
and published several works on that subject. ‡

---

* Anatomy of a pigmy, compared with a monkey,
an ape, and a man; and a philological essay concerning pigmies, cynocephali, satyrs, and sphynxes,
1699, 4to. Also 1751, with various papers of the
author from the Philosophical Transactions.

† Osservazioni Anatomiche intorno alle Tartarughe
maritime, d'aqua dolce, e terrestri, Firenze, 1687,
4to.

‡ Historiæ Animalium tres Tractatus, Lond. 1678,

The foundation of the Royal Society in this country, and of the Royal Academy of Sciences in Paris, constituted an era very favourable to the advancement of natural knowledge. The voluminous transactions* of both these learned societies, abound from their commencement with valuable information on the structure and functions of animals. Similar associations formed sooner or later in all the principal states of Europe, turned men's minds to the proper method of observation and ex-

4to. Exercitatio Anatomica de Cochleis et Limacibus, 1694. Exercitatio altera de Buccinis, 1695. Exercit. Tertia Conchyliorum Bivalvium, 1696.

* The Transactions of the French Academy, under the title of Histoire et Memoires de l'Acad. Royale des Sciences, with the tables, &c. fiom its establishment in 1666 to its dissolution at the French revolution, constitute a series of 163 volumes, 4to. The Memoires de l'Institut form a continuation to the present time.

periment, diffused a general taste for natural knowledge, and collected copious materials for its advancement. The society of Naturæ Curiosi in Germany,* the academies of Petersburgh,† Stockholm,‡ Berlin,§ Goet-

---

* The papers published by this body occupy between 40 and 50 volumes, under the various titles of Miscellanea, seu Ephemerides Medico-physici; Ephemerid. seu obs. Medico-phys.; acta Physico-med. and nova acta.

† The Commentarii Academiæ Scientiarium Imperialis Petropolitanæ, the Novi Commentarii, Acta, Nova Acta, and Memoires, consist of 64 vols. 4to. to the year 1810.

‡ The Transactions of the Stockholm Academy are published in Swedish, and translated into German, under the title of Abhandlungen der Königlichen Schwedischen Akademie, &c. 8vo.

§ Miscellanea Berolinensia, and Histoire de l'Acad. Royale des Sciences, avec les Memoires.

E

tingen,* and Bologna,† are the most important of these; but there have been many minor establishments. ‡

A very noble work was begun and prosecuted for some time by the French aca-

---

* Commentarii, novi Commentarii, et Commentationes Regiæ Societatis Scientiarum Goettingensis; 4to.

† Commentarii de Bononiensi Scientiarum et Artium instituto atque Academia, 4to.

‡ Two valuable but very rare volumes were published by a private association at Amsterdam, and relate principally to comparative anatomy. Observationes Anatomicæ selectiores Collegii privati Amstelodamensis, 1667 and 1673; 2 t. 12mo.

Associations for the advancement of natural knowledge have also existed at Copenhagen, Upsal, Haerlem, Flushing, Rotterdam, Münich, Turin, Verona, Florence, Siena, &c. and have published their transactions in various languages.

demicians (principally Perrault* and Duverney;† Mery‡ and Philip de la Hire were
also concerned);—a complete history of
animals, founded on original observations
and dissections, particularly of the rarer

---

* Besides the share which he had in the work mentioned above, Perrault discusses some points in the
structure of animals in his Essais de Physique, 4 t.
4to.

† Jos. Guichard Duverney, professor of anatomy at
Paris, spent nearly sixty years in dissection, and is the
author of a vast number of papers in the early Memoirs of the Academy of Sciences, relating to the
structure of animals, as well as of man. There is
also some comparative anatomy in the second volume
of his Œuvres Anatomiques, 1761, 2 t. 4to. a posthumous work.

‡ Many papers on the anatomy of animals by this
industrious anatomist are found in the Memoirs of the
Academy of Sciences; among them an account of
transplanting the spur of a cock to the head, where it
adhered. Ann. 1688.

species, that were kept in the menageries of Louis XIV. The descriptions were first published separately, but were after- . wards collected into a magnificent folio volume under the title of Memoires pour servir a l'Histoire Naturelle des Animaux. 1671; they were re-published with additions in two volumes in 1676. In this work, which has been also printed in quarto,* and translated into English and Latin, we have excellent descriptions, among other animals, of the elephant, camel, beaver, bear, gazelle, lion, tiger, panther, civette, of the crocodile and

---

* Paris, 1733. Amsterdam, 1758, 3 tom. under the title " Memoires pour servir à l'Histoire Naturelle des Animaux, dressès par Mr. Perrault." To the third part is added the description of the viper by Charas, and of the crocodile and some other foreign animals by the Jesuit missionaries at Siam.

camelion, of the bustard, stork, crane, flamingo, and vulture.

The work of Blasius, entitled Anatomia Animalium figuris variis illustrata, is principally a collection of the contributions to comparative anatomy that appeared in the seventeenth century.   It contains the dissections of numerous animals made by the best naturalists of those times, and may still be deemed a useful compilation.   Collins's System of Anatomy in two vols. folio, Lond. 1685, contains numerous dissections and delineations of the parts of animals, particularly of fishes and birds.

The eighteenth century will be ever memorable for the advancement, not only of general civilization, but of all branches of knowledge; and the structure and functions of animals have experienced their full share of this progress. I can only notice the more important contributors. The formation of shells,* and of the hard covering of the crustaceous animals,† as the crab, lobster, &c. ; the anatomy and habits of various testaceous mollusca,‡ or

---

* De la Formation et de l'accroissement des Coquilles, des Animaux, tant terrestres qu' aquatiques, &c. Mem. de l'Acad. des Sciences, 1709.

Eclaircissement de quelques difficultés sur la formation et l'accroissement des Coquilles ; ibid. 1716.

† Sur les diverses reproductions, qui se font dans les ecrevisses, les omars, les crabes, &c. et entr'autres sur celle de leurs jambes, et de leurs Ecailles. Ibid. 1712.

Additions aux Observations sur la mue des Ecrevissés données dans les Mem. de 1712. Ibid, 1718.

There is also a memoir on the same subject, by Mr. Geoffroy, Jun.; Observations sur les Ecrevisses de riviere. Ibid, 1709.

‡ Du Mouvement progressif et de quelques autres

shell-fish as they are called, and the history of insects, * have been investigated with great success, and most happily described by Reaumur,† more generally known by

---

Mouvemens de diverses Especes de Coquillages, orties, et Etoiles de Mer.   Ibid, 1710.

Des differentes Manieres, dont plusieurs Especes d'Animaux de mer s'attachent au sable, aux pierres, et les uns aux autres.   Ibid, 1711.

Observations sur le Mouvement progressif de quelques Coquillages de mer, sur celui des hérissons de mer, &c.   Ibid, 1712.

Observations sur le Coquillage appelé Pinne Marine, ou nacre de Perle.   Ibid, 1717.

* Memoires pour servir a l'Histoire Naturelle des Insectes; 6 t. 4to. 1734—1742.

† He also published some excellent experiments on the digestion of birds in the Academy of Sciences, 1752; and a work by no means destitute of physiological interest, entitled, art de faire Eclorre et d'Elever en

the invention of the thermometer, which
bears his name. The works of Bonnet, *
Rœsel, † De Geer, ‡ Merian, § and Sulzer,‖

---

toute saison des oiseaux domestiques, &c. 2 t. 12mo.
1749.

* Traitè d'insectologie, 1745. Other parts of his
works relate to the structure and physiology of animals:
they were published in 8 vols. 4to.; and 18 v. 8vo.
1779.

† Monatlich-herausgegebene Insecten-belustigun-
gen; with coloured plates; 4to. Nüremberg, with
a continuation by Kleeman; forming together 4 vols.
4to. 1746—1761. The third volume contains an account of some crustacea and a most interesting history
of the fresh water polypes.

‡ Memoires pour servir a l'Histoire Naturelle
des Insectes, 4to.; Stockholm, 1752—1758.

§ De Generatione et Metamorphosibus insectorum
Surinamensium; Hag. fol. 1726.

‖ Geschichte der Insecten. Winterthur, 1775, 4to.

contain much information on the structure
and functions, as well as the natural history
of insects; and the anatomy of the larva
of the phalæna cossus by Lyonet, * is a
chef d'œuvre both of anatomical research
and of the art of engraving. The recent
researches of Huber † on the bee and ant
have unfolded to us many surprising circumstances in the physiology and habits
of those insects.

, In the list of those, who have employed
themselves in observing the minuter parts
of the animal kingdom, we must not omit
the name of Trembley, ‡ whose history of

---

* Traitè Anatomique de la Chenille, qui ronge le
bois de Saule, 4to. a la Haye, 1762.

† Nouvelles Observations sur les Abeilles : translated into English, 12mo. 1806. Recherches sur les
mœurs des fourmis indigenes; 1810.

‡ Memoire pour servir à l'Histoire d'un genre de
Polypes, &c. Leid. 1744, 4to.

the fresh water polypes and their almost
miraculous properties, by strongly interesting the public attention, and exciting
a spirit of inquiry, may be considered as
forming an era in zoology. He made us
acquainted with animals, which propagate
by shoots, like those of the vegetable
kingdom, the young one budding out from
the body of its parent, expanding, and
separating when fully unfolded, and some-
times producing new shoots before it is
detached; which, when cut into two or
more pieces, form quickly so many perfect
animals; of which two, when cut and

See also Baker's Natural History of the Polype.
Lond. 1743, 8vo.

Roesel Historie der Polypen in the 3d vol. of his
Insecten Belustigungen.

Schœffer's Armpolypen in der Süssen Wassern um
Regensburg; 1754, 4to.

applied to each other, grow together, forming a single animal, with a head at each
end.   When slit longitudinally through
half their length, each portion forms a
perfect head; by repeating this process,
a kind of hydra may be formed with many
heads joined to a single tail.   It may be
turned inside out without injury; and may
even be turned back-again.

The Linnæan class Vermes has been
principally illustrated by Bohadsch, *
Pallas,† Müller,‡ Forskaohl,§ and Po-

---

* De quibusdam Animalıbus marinis, &c.   Dresd.
1761, 4to.   De veris sepiarum ovis. Prag. 1752.

† Miscellanea Zoologica et Spicilegia Zoologica.

‡ Historia vermium terrestrium et Fluviatilium,
2 t. 4to. Havniæ, 1773 and 1774.

Icones Zoologiæ Danicæ, ibid, 1777, et seq. fol.

Animalcula Infusoria fluviatilia et marina, &c. 4to.
Havniæ, 1786.

§ Icones rerum Naturalium, quas ex itinere Orientali
depingi Curavit; Edente C. Niebuhr. Havniæ, 1776, fol.

li.* The mechanism of animal motions, already considered at great length, by Borelli,† has been further illustrated by Barthez.‡

In collecting the materials of the grand work, which will immortalize the name of Buffon,§ its eloquent author was assisted by Daubenton, who had the charge of the collection established at the Jardin des Plantes, and who contributed the anatomical descriptions; not the least important part of this noble undertaking. These

---

* Testacea utriusque Siciliæ, eorumque Historia et Anatome, 1791. Parma, 2 v. fol.

† De motu Animalium, 2 v. 4to.

‡ Nouvelle mechanique des Mouvemens de l'Homme et des Animaux, Carcassone, 1798, 4to.

§ See Eloge de Buffon par Condorcet; also by Vicq. D'azyr, in his Œuvres, t. 1.

are found only in the original quarto
edition ; * they are omitted at least in the
greatest part of the numerous subsequent
editions.   Vicq d'Azyr was formed by the
instructions and example of Daubenton,
and displayed that ardent love of science,
that patience in research, and those philosophic views, which qualified him to have
carried comparative anatomy to its highest
pitch of perfection.   Although he was cut
off in the flower of his age by a premature
death, he has left behind him sufficient

---

* Histoire Naturelle generale et particuliere, avec
la Description du Cabinet du roi, Paris, 4to. 1750 et
suiv.

There are also several papers by Daubenton in the
Memoires de l'Acad. des Sciences, from 1751 to 1760.

See Discours sur la vie et les Ouvrages, &c. de Daubenton, a l'ouverture des cours d'Histoire Naturelle
au Museum, l'an 8, par Lacepede ; et Notice sur la
vie et les Ouvrages de Daubenton par Cuvier.

proofs that this eulogy is not exagge-
rated *.

The talents and the merits of Camper
and Pallas are universally recognised :
their works are copious sources of information on the most important and interesting
parts of comparative anatomy. Those of
the former, which have relation to our present subject, are collected in a French
edition, in 3 volumes, 8vo. with folio
plates †. The principal productions of
Pallas are his Miscellanea Zoologica, Spicilegia Zoologiæ, and Novæ Species Quad-
rupedum. He has, besides, contributed

---

* Œuvres, recueillies, par J. Moreau de la Sarthe,
5 tom. 8vo. avec un Atlas, in 4to. 1805.

† Œuvres de P. Camper, qui ont pour Objet
l'Histoire naturelle, la Physiologie, et l'Anatomie
comparée. Paris, 1803.

several zoological papers to the Petersburg transactions, and has scattered much information on detached points through the instructive narratives of his travels in the various provinces of the Russian empire.

In the immortal work of Haller, the Elementa Physiologiæ, which, from the extensive field it embraces, its copious materials, both of original research and erudition; its luminous arrangement, and perspicuous style; as well as the sound judgment and acute reasoning displayed throughout, we can have no difficulty in characterizing as by far the most valuable book in medical science: there is a complete collection of all the facts ascertained previously to his time concerning the structure and functions of animals, with several additions from his own observation. I earnestly recommend this work to the attentive perusal of my younger hearers—not only as an inexhaustible mine of physiological information, but on account of the ardent love of science, and the philosophic spirit which animate every page.

Blumenbach, who succeeded him in the school of Göttingen, has exhibited in 'the cultivation of zoology great industry, acutenes, and sound judgment, and has enriched his favourite science with excellent elementary works. In his admirable Treatise* on the varieties of the human species, he has touched on several interesting points of comparative structure and physiology. The same remark is applicable to his Essay on Generation†, and to

---

* De generis humani varietate nativa; Götting. 1775; 3d edition, 1795.

† Ueber den Bildungstrieb, 12mo. Götting. 1791. Translated into English by Dr. Crichton.

his description of the bones*. He has
not only published an admirable manual
of natural history†, particularly valuable
for the anatomical and physiological information with which it abounds, but has
annually delivered, for many years a full

---

* Geschichte und Beschreibung der Knochen des
Menschlichen Körpers, Götting. 1786.

† Handbuch der Naturgeschichte, 6th edition,
Gotting. 1799. There is, I believe, a more recent
edition It has been translated into French, under
the title of Manuel d'Histoire Naturelle; and it is to
be regretted that we have not an English version of
this concise and perspicuous, yet comprehensive and
philosophic work. It is by far the best introduction to
natural history in any language. The Abbildungen
Natur-historischer Gegenstände, Gött. 8vo. 1796—
1810, contains a well selected and valuable series of
engravings of interesting subjects in natural history.
Ten parts are published, containing each ten engravings.

course of lectures on comparative anatomy in the University of Göttingen. His compendium of Comparative Anatomy * was principally designed as a text book for those lectures; and it contains, on every point, copious references to the best sources of information. His tract, entitled, Specimen Physiologiæ comparatæ inter animalia calidi et frigidi sanguinis; Gött. 4to. 1789, is an interesting essay on the physiology of reptiles.

The Treatise of Scarpa on the Organs of Smelling and Hearing†, and the great work

---

* A second edition of the Handbuch der Vergleichenden Anatomie was published in 1815.

† Disquisitiones Anatomicæ de Auditu & Olfactu, fol. 2d edition, Milan, 1795. See also his work, De Structura fenestræ rotundæ auris. There is another work on the same subject by an Italian anatomist;

of Poli already noticed, on the testaceous animals of the two Sicilies, deserve our highest praise for their anatomical accuracy, and for the singular beauty of their numerous engravings.

Their countryman Spallanzani devoted himself with enthusiastic ardour to the cultivation of natural history; not to a barren and wearisome science of nomenclature and external forms; but to the philosophic investigation, by observation and experiment, of the origin, functions, and habits of living beings. The generation of animals and of plants, the circulation of the blood, respiration, digestion, the reproduction of parts in certain classes, seminal animalcula, and the ani-

Comparetti Observationes Anatomicæ de aure interna comparata; 4to. Patav. 1789.

mals of infusions, were the subjects of an almost incredible number of researches and experiments.   IIis writings * afford

* Saggio di Osservazioni Microscopiche concernente il Sistema della Generazione dei S. Needham é Buffon, 1765.

Dei fenomeni della Circolazione, &c.   Modena, 1773.

Prodromo di un opera da imprimersi sopra le Riproduzioni Animali.   1768.

Opuscoli de fisica Animale é Vegetabile, t. 1 and 2, 1776; t. 3 and 4, 1780.

Lettera sopra il sospetto d'un nuovo senso nei Pipis-trelli.

Mèmoires sur la Respiration, traduites en François d'après les MSS. inedits de l'auteur.   Par J. Sennebier.   8vo. Geneva.

Rapports de l'air avec les êtres Organisés, tirès des Journaux de Spallanzani, &c.   Par J. Sennebier. Ge-neva, 1807. 3 vols.   Of the foregoing works, the 2d, 4th, and 6th, have been translated into English.   An interesting account of the author's life is prefixed to the Mem. sur la Respiration.

abundant original information on all these points, and amply justify the expressive eulogium of Haller, " summus naturæ in minimis indagator."   Founded entirely on actual observation, dictated merely by the desire to unfold the operations of nature, and executed with clearness and simplicity, they interest the reader very powerfully; while they are not less valuable as sources of useful information.   They have accordingly been translated into almost all the modern European languages.

The works of Pallas *, Bloch †, Goeze ‡,

---

* De infestis viventibus intra viventia.   Leid. 1760, 4to.

† Traité de la Generation des vers Intestins, &c. Strasburg, 1788, 8vo.   The original was published in German. Berlin, 1782, 4to.

‡ Versuch Einer Naturgeschichte der Eingeweide-

Zeder*, Werner†, and Rudolphi‡, have nearly completed the anatomy and natural history of internal worms.

Sulzer has given us an excellent account of a single animal, the hamster§, (Mar-

---

würmer thierischer Körper; Blankenburg, 1782, 4to. mit 44 Kupfern.

Erster Nachtrag zur Naturgeschichte der Eingeweidewürmer, Von J. A. Goeze, mit Zusätzen und bemerkungen herausgegeben, Von J. G. H. Zeder; Leipsic, 1800.

* Anleitung zur Naturgeschichte der Eingeweidewürmer. Von J. G. H. Zeder. Bamberg, 1803, 8vo.

† Vermium intestinalium, præsertim tæniæ humanæ, brevis Expositio; Lips. 1782, 8vo. and continuation in three parts, 1782 et seq.

‡ Entozoorum seu Vermium Intestinalium Historia Naturalis. 2 t. 8vo. Amsterd. 1808 and 9.

§ Versuch einer Naturgeschichto des Hamsters: Götting. 1774. 8vo.

mota Cricetus, Linn.): and Roesel* has devoted a folio volume in the Latin and German languages to the anatomy and natural history of the frog and toad kind,

---

* Historia Naturalis Ranarum nostratium; Nuremberg, 1758, fol. with a preface by Haller. See also, on subjects nearly connected with this, Mr. Hunter's Anatomy of the Siren Lacertina from Carolina. Philos. Transact v. 56, p. 307 et seq.

Schreiber's Anatomy and Natural History of the Proteus Anguinus from Carniola, ibid. 1801, p. 2.

And a masterly account by Cuvier, not only of the two animals just mentioned (the Siren and Proteus), but also of the tadpoles of different frogs and salamanders, drawn up with his accustomed accuracy and acuteness; Recherches Anatomiques sur les Reptiles regardés encore comme douteux par les Naturalistes, faites a l'occasion de l'axolotl rapporté par M. de Humboldt du Mexique, 1807, 4to. It forms part of the Recueil d'Observations de Zoologie & d'Anatomie comparée of Humboldt.

which subjects he has prosecuted with the greatest accuracy and minuteness, and illustrated with a vast·number of beautiful coloured plates.

The Jardin des Plantes, and its superb Zoological cabinet, have been employed by the French naturalists in a manner that shews them worthy of the treasure—worthy of succeeding to Buffon, Daubenton, and Vicq D'Azyr. Their zeal and exertions, abundantly evinced in the twenty volumes of Annals of the Museum of Natural History, which have been completed within a few years, and constitute one of the most valuable accessions, that zoology has ever received, have given an impulse to the cultivation of natural knowledge, which will form a most important æra in its history. To estimate its effect, it will be sufficient to recount the names,

and to recall the instructive works of Lacepede *, Latreille †, Lamarck ‡, Geoffroy
St. Hilaire§, Daudin‖, Brongniart, Peron¶,

* Histoire Naturelle des Cetacès, 1 t. 4to. Hist.
Nat. des Quadrupédes ovipares et des Serpens, 2 t.
4to.; and Hist. Nat. des Poissons, 4 t. 4to. published
as a continuation of Buffon.

† Hist. Nat. des Insectes; des Salamandres de
France, &c.

‡ Système des Animaux sans vertebres.

§ Various papers in the Annales du Museum.

‖ Hist. Nat. des Reptiles.

¶ Voyage aux terres Australes; enriched with copious zoological remarks, and beautiful coloured plates.
Sur le genre Pyrosoma; Annales du Museum, t. 4,
p. 437.

Sur les Meduses du genre Equorée; ibid. t. 15.
Sur la Famille des mollusques pteropodes. Ibid. Sur
l'Habitation des animaux marins, et des Phoques.
Ibid. The very extraordinary zeal and activity displayed by Peron in the pursuit of zoology, and parti-

Dumeril*, Cuvier †.   Every part of the
wide field of Zoology has been survey-

---

cularly his unremitting and severe labours in the
voyage of discovery sent by the French government to
New Holland and the adjacent countries, in which he
procured himself a commission by his scientific ardour
and importunity, after the full complement of naturalists had been already named, and from which he
brought back, in conjunction with his associate Le
Sueur, above 100,000 specimens of the animal kingdom, and more than 2500 new species, lead us to
deplore his early death as a severe loss to science.
See Notice Historique sur M. Peron, par M. Deleuze;
Annales du Mus. t. 17, p. 352, et seq.

Also, Eloge de Peron, par Alard, in the Societé
Medicale d'Emulation, t. 7.

* Zoologie Analytique, 8vo. Paris, 1806.

† Much valuable information on comparative anatomy may be derived from the following French collections, viz.: Ménagerie du Muséum National, fol.
Bulletin des Sciences.   Memoires de la Societe d'Hist.
Natuielle de Paris.

ed by the latter enlightened and zealous inquirer, and no corner has escaped his penetrating glance. Equal to Buffon in enlarged views and comprehensive grasp of mind, and much superior to him in patient research, minute observation, and learned inquiry, he presents a rare union of all the great requisites for promoting natural knowledge. He has been not less fortunate in his situation, than in his qualifications; devoting his whole time to science, and surrounded by numerous able assistants, he could avail himself, to their full extent, of those liberal institutions for the advancement of natural knowledge, and that uniform encouragement of talent, for which science will ever be indebted to the late French government. Accordingly his progress has been every where marked by improvement and discovery. I select one or two principal points from the multitude of his researches*. In a long series of papers †, printed in the Annals of the Na-

---

* His interesting labours on the larynx of birds ought not however to pass unnoticed. See Magazin Encyclopédique; an. 1, t. 2, and an. 4, t. 2.

See also, on the subject of the vocal organs, Girardi in Memorie della Società Italiana, t. 2, p. 2.

Hérissant in Mem. de l'Acad. des Sciences, 1753.

M. J. Busch Diss. de Mechanismo Organi Vocis, Groning. 1770, 4to.

Vicq d'Azyr in the Acad. des Sciences, 1779. Wolff Diss. Anatomica de Organo Vocis Mammalium; Berolini, 1812, 4to.

Latham in Transactions of the Linnæan Society, vol. 4.

† Sur l'Animal de la Lingule (Lingula Anatina. Lamarck). Annales du Mus. Nat. de l'Hist. Naturelle, t. 1. p. 69.

Sur la Bullæa Aperta (Lamarck), Bulla Aperta (Linn.) ibid. p. 156.

tional Museum of Natural History, and
presenting models of clear and precise de-

Sur le clio Borealis; ib. 242.

Sur le genre Tritonia, avec la Description et l'Anat.
d'un genre nouvelle, Tritonia Hombergii; ib. 480.

Sur le genre Aplysia, Vulgairement nommé lievre
marin; sur son Anatomie, et quelques unes de ses
especes; t. 2, p. 287.

Sur l'Animal de l'Hyale, sur un nouveau genre de
Mollusques nus, intermediaire entre l'hyale et le clio,
&c.; t. 4. p. 223.

Sur les Thalides (Thalia Brown.) et sur les Bi-
phores (Salpa Forskaohl.) t. 4. p. 360.

Sur le genre Doris; ib. 447.

Sur l'Onchidie, genre de Mollusques nus voisin des
limaces, et sur une espece nouvelle, onchidium Pe-
ronii; t. 5, p. 37.

Sur la Phyllidie, et le Pleurobranche, deux nou-
veaux genres de mollusques de la Famille des gasteropodes, dont l'un est nu, et dont l'autre porte une
coquille molle; ibid. 5, 266.

scription, he has perfected the. anatomy of
the mollusca, hitherto hardly begun, illus-

Sur la Dolabelle, la Testacelle, et un nouveau
genre de Mollusques a coquille cachée, nommé Par-
macelle; ibid. 435.

Sur la Scyllée, l'Eolide, et le Glaucus, avec des
Additions au Memoire sur la Tritonie, t. 6, p. 416.

Sur le limace, et le colimacon, t. 7. 140.

Sur le limnée (helix stagnalis, Linn.) et le planorbe,
(hel. cornea, Linn.) ibid. 185.

Sur l'Ianthine et la phasianelle de Mr. Lamarck;
t. 11. p. 121.

Sur la vivipare d'eau douce (cyclostoma viviparum
Draparnaud; Helix vivip. Linn.); sur quelques espece voisines, &c. ibid. 170.

Sur le grand buccin de nos côtes, (buccinum unda-
tum, Linn.) ainsi que sur les buccins, les murex, les
strombus, et en general sur les gasteropodes pectinés
à syphon; ibid. 447.

Sur le genre Tethys, et son Anatomie; t. 12, 257.

trating them by a vast number of most
beautiful and expressive figures engraved
from his own drawings, and clearing away
the confusion in which the species and
genera had been hitherto involved. His
examination of fossil bones presents a singular combination of most extensive, laborious, and minute investigation, with grand
and astonishing results.   Having collected
a vast number of specimens, mostly mutilated, he examined them carefully, compared them with each other, and drew

---

Sur les Acères, ou gasteropodes sans tentacules
apparens; t. 16, p. 1.

Sur les Ascidies, et sur leur Anatomie ; Mémoires
du Muséum d'Hist. Nat. t. 2, p. 10.

Sur les Animaux des anatifes et des balanes Lam.
(Lepas. Linn.), et sur leur Anatomie, ibid. p. 85.

All these papers are illustrated with numerous most
expressive and beautiful engravings from Cuvier's
drawings.

them. He studied minutely the corresponding bones of the analogous known
species of animals. From these comparisons he was enabled to decide that the
fossil bones are for the most part different
from those of any existing creatures, and
consequently that they belonged to races
of animals that have disappeared from our
globe; or at least of whose existence in
the living state neither history nor tradi-
tion afford any traces.

" Engaged," says he, " in antiquarian
researches of a new kind, I have been
obliged to learn the art of deciphering and
restoring these monuments, of recognising
and replacing in their primitive arrangement the scattered and mutilated fragments
of which they consist; of reconstructing
those ancient beings, to which they belonged; of exhibiting their proportions and
characters; and lastly, of comparing them

to those, which are found at this moment on the surface of the globe: an art almost unknown, and presupposing the existence of a science hitherto almost untouched, I mean the laws of co-existence, which regulate the forms of the various parts of organized beings. I could only prepare myself for these researches by much longer researches on existing animals. It was necessary to review almost the whole of the present creation in order to give the force of demonstration to my conclusions respecting this extinct creation. This review produced numerous rules and relations of a character not less demonstrative; and I thus discovered new laws applicable to the whole animal kingdom, on occasion of this inquiry into a small part of the theory of the earth.*"

* Sur les Ossemens Fossiles; Discours Preliminaire.

G

He has succeeded in distinguishing the
fossil remains of seventy-eight species of
animals, many of them of the largest size.
Forty-nine of these are certainly unknown
to naturalists to the present time: eleven
or twelve resemble known species so closely, that we cannot doubt their identity.
The sixteen or eighteen that remain are
still exposed to some doubt; so that it is
not yet determined whether or no they
are the same with any present species.
These researches, originally published in
detached papers in the Annals of the Museum of Natural History, have since been
collected in 4 vols. 4to. which not only
contain the grandest and most striking
discovery yet made in Comparative Anatomy, or in Geology, but offer the most
unexceptionable model for the manner in
which the inquiry has been conducted,
the cautious philosophic reasoning displayed in every branch of it, and the

satisfactory clearness with which the conclusions are established.

Thus the same objects, which when
viewed in an isolated manner, and super-
ficially examined, had given rise to the
belief in the former existence of giants and
monsters, afforded in the hands of a philosopher who contemplated them with all
the auxiliary lights of modern science, the
means of dissipating many absurd fables,
and of establishing a conclusion not only
the most important hitherto made, concerning the construction of the globe which
we inhabit, but equally valuable as an instrument of criticism in estimating the hypotheses of geology, and in weighing the pro-
bability of the traditions that relate to the
early history and past condition of our
earth.   " The latter subject, which is the
ultimate term of all these researches, is one
of the most curious that can engage our

attention. If we feel an interest in following, through the infancy of our species, the almost effaced traces of so many extinct nations, we shall be at least equally gratified in exploring, amid the darkness that involves the early ages of the earth, the remains of revolutions anterior to the existence of all nations."*

That geology should have derived its most important accession from comparative anatomy—that the history of the globe should have been elucidated by the examination of some fragments of bones, is a striking illustration of the connexion between the different sciences, and of the aid which they are capable of affording each other. It shews us that little can be expected from the exclusive prosecution of

* Ibid.

one; and that a man who wishes to succeed signally in any branch of knowledge, should have his mind fortified by the possession of many branches.

In his capacity of professor of the anatomy of animals, Cuvier has for many years delivered lectures at the Jardin des Plantes, where the number of his audience (often exceeding a thousand) sufficiently proves the ability of the teacher, and the interest inspired by the subject.   His lectures, collected by some of his young assistants, and revised by himself, constitute the most comprehensive and philosophic production that has yet appeared on comparative anatomy : I might say on zoology. But these five volumes are only an epitome or rather prospectus of a much more extensive labour on the same subject; in which the acknowledged genius and industry, not less than the vast acquirements and the splendid performances of the author, lead us to expect, that the foundations of zoology will be so firmly laid in the materials derived from comparative anatomy and physiology, that the edifice will be secure from time and accident, and perpetuate the fame of Cuvier as equal, if not superior to any zoologist that has hitherto appeared.

I ought not to omit mentioning to you his Tableau Elementaire d'Histoire Naturelle, as a very useful compendium of natural history.

Having noticed the public establishments, in a neighbouring nation, devoted to the cultivation of natural history; having observed the powerful impulse which they have given to that department of knowledge, and paid the just tribute of gratitude to the French zoologists;---I return to our own country, and am ashamed to find, that although her colonies and commercial establishments are found in every region and every climate, while every sea is covered and every coast is visited by her ships, these great facilities have been as greatly neglected. We have no national collection of living animals, no museum of natural history, no public institution for teaching natural science.

" Pudet hæc opprobria nobis,
Et dici potuisse, et non potuisse refelli."

That the monastic institutions of a barbarous age should contain no provisions for teaching natural science, will not be a matter of wonder, because natural science did not then exist : these establishments were at least calculated for teaching according to the measure of knowledge at the period of their institution. But what excuse shall we find for the modern *universities* as they are called, of a nation which fancies itself the most enlightened in Europe? *universities*, which totally neglect natural history and all its connected pursuits, as if they were no part of *universal* knowledge.

The necessary consequence is, that Zoological pursuits have languished in England during great part of the past century. Yet we can justly claim the merit of some important discoveries. Mr. Hewson*, the surgeon, demonstrated the lymphatics in birds, fishes, and reptiles; thus completing the great physiological doctrine of the absorbing system, which had been already fully established in the human subject, by his illustrious master, William Hunter, also a member of the corporation of Sur-

* Philosophical Transactions, v. 58 and 59. Also, Experimental Inquiries on the Blood, p. 1 and 2.

geons. Ellis proved that the Zoophytes, hitherto regarded as plants, belong to the animal kingdom; and shewed the minute animals which form or inhabit these productions*.

The excellent work and the beautiful plates of Stubbs, on the Anatomy of the Horse, should not be omitted; nor the engravings, which he was publishing just before his death, containing a comparative view of the human structure with those of the cock and tiger.

Although they belong more to natural history than to comparative anatomy, I

* Natural History of Corallines, London, 1755, 4to. Natural History of many curious and uncommon Zoophytes, &c. arranged by Dr. Solander, 1786, 4to. See also, on the same subject, Fil. Cavolini, Memorie per servire alla Storia de' polipi marini, Nap. 1785, 4to.

am unwilling to omit mentioning the very
ingenious and interesting researches of Mr.
Bracy Clark, on the Genus Œstrus, first
published in the third volume of the
Linnæan Transactions, p. 289 et seq. as
" Observations on the Genus Œstrus ;"
and separately republished, with additions,
in the present year, with the title, " On
the Bots of Horses," in 4to. The very
extraordinary history of a singular tribe of
insects is satisfactorily made out from
actual observation, in this Essay ; and the
confusion, in which most of the species
were involved is dispelled.

Monro's Structure and Physiology of
Fishes (fol. Edinb. 1785) deserves remark, as almost the only contribution
to comparative anatomy from the northern part of this island. Although in re-
presenting scientific objects, the execu-
tion of engravings is subordinate to their
fidelity, there can be no sufficient reason

for the singular coarseness of those which accompany this volume, forming a contras to the highly beautiful specimens exhibited in the works of Sœmmerring and Scarpa, not very honourable to the arts of this country.

Mr. Carlisle's papers, in the Philosophical Transactions*, display a degree of ingenuity and talent, which make us regret that his contributions have not been more numerous; and that science has lost the benefit of those acquisitions, which must have resulted, had he employed his acute mind on some subjects of suitable importance in comparative anatomy or physiology.

* On a peculiar distribution of the Arteries of the Extremities in Slow-moving Animals, 1800. On the Stapes, 1805. On the Arrangement and Mechanical Action of the Muscles of Fishes, 1806.

But Mr. Hunter is the glory of England in this century. In vigour and originality of genius, in comprehension and depth of thought, in unwearied industry, he has been surpassed by none. He was one of the men who give a character to the age in which they live—whose names are associated to the great æras of science—and who do honour to the country which produces them. Occupied by a laborious profession, and defraying from its hard earnings the expences of his multifarious inquiries, he accomplished what appears almost incredible. What might he not have done, had his time been devoted exclusively to his favourite pursuits, and had they been aided by that pecuniary assistance and fostering support, which the rulers of mankind so seldom and so unwillingly spare from their schemes of war and conquest. He surveyed anatomy and physiology with the eye of a philosopher; proceeding constantly, with the aid of dissection and experiment, to ascertain the structure of animals, and to determine the nature of their functions.   There is scarcely a branch of physiology, which he has not illustrated by some original researches; while he has examined each organ in every animal that he could procure*.   His Museum is arranged on this truly philosophic principle; a plan followed by Aristotle, and to be completed, I hope, by Cuvier. His equal or even greater merits in the elucidation of disease do not belong to

* The Hunterian collection contains abundant memorials of these labours.   Besides what has been given to the public in his posthumous work on the Blood, and in the collection of papers on the Animal Economy, there is an account of the electrical Organs of the Torpedo in the Philos. Trans. for 1773; of the Silurus Electricus in the Trans. 1775 ; and of the Anatomy of Whales in the same work, 1787.

the present subject; and it is the less necessary to mention them, as they have
been so recently enforced and illustrated
in this theatre by a kindred genius.

The bust of Hunter could not have
been more appropriately placed, than in
the collection, which is the pride and boast
of this College, and universally allowed to
be unrivalled for the number, beauty, and
value of its specimens. The surrounding
labour of his own hands forms the most
suitable memorial of that great man; were
an inscription required to characterize him,
I would borrow the short but expressive
one from the tomb of a great artist, placed
in one of his principal works;

" Si monumentum quæras, circumspice."

Sir Everard Hume, to whom we are not
less indebted for upholding the scientific

character of our profession, than for raising
and maintaining its rank in society, and
who first delivered lectures on comparative
anatomy in this Theatre, enjoyed the rare
advantage of being initiated in anatomy
and physiology under the guidance of
Hunter. Though he has directed his pursuits to various parts of comparative anatomy, the results of which are contained in
numerous interesting papers * published in
the Philosophical Transactions, his principal

* Anatomy of the sea otter, Phil. Trans. 1796, p. 2.

Anatomy of the ornithorhynchus paradoxus, and
hystrix; ibid, 1800, p. 2; 1802, p. 1 and 2.

On the mode of generation of the kanguroo; ib:d,
1795, p. 2.

On the expansion of the skin of the neck in the
cobra de capello; ibid, 1804, p. 2.

On the progressive motion of snakes; ibid, 1812,
p. 1.

attention has been bestowed on the teeth,*

Account of some peculiarities in the anatomical structure of the wombat; with observations on the female organs of generation ; 1808, p. 2.

On the mode of breeding of the ovoviviparous shark, and on the aeration of the fœtal blood in different classes of animals; 1810, p. 2.

On the fossil remains of an animal allied to fishes; 1814, p. 2.

On the organs of respiration in some fishes and vermes; 1815, p. 2.

On the organs of generation of the lamprey and myxine ; ibid.

* Observations on the teeth of graminivorous quadrupeds, particularly those of the elephant and sus æthiopicus. Philos. Trans. 1799, p. 2.

Observations on the structure and mode of growth of the teeth of the wild boar and animal incognitum ; ibid, 1801, p. 2.

See also on the same subject;

the stomach, * and the rest of the alimentary canal. The lectures,† which

---

Mr. Corse's observations on the different species of Asiatic elephants, and their mode of dentition; ibid, 1799, p. 2.

Blake's Essay on the structure and formation of the teeth in man, and various animals; Dublin, 8vo. 1801.

Tenon sur une methode particuliere d'etudier l'anatomie; Mem. de l'Institut National, t. 1, an. 6. On the teeth of the horse.

Cuvier in the Recherches sur les ossemens fossiles des Quadrupedes, t. 2, p. 67, et seq. for an admirable account of the dentition of the elephant. It was first published in his Mémoire sur les especes d'Elephans vivantes et fossiles, in the Memoires de l'Institut. an. 7.

Broussonet memoire sur les dents de l'homme, et des autres animaux comparés entr'eux; Mem. de l'Acad. des Sciences, 1787.

* Different papers on this subject, which first appeared in the Philosophical Transactions, are reprinted in the lectures mentioned below.

† Lectures on Comparative Anatomy, in which are illustrated the preparations in the Hunterian collection;

he delivered in this chair, and has since
published at the request of the curators
of the Museum, are arranged on the best
principles of philosophical zoology, and
illustrated by an extremely valuable series
of figures engraved from the expressive and
beautiful drawings of Mr. Clift.

To my immediate predecessor, this college and the public are indebted for the
zeal and industry with which he executed
his task, and the great mass of original
materials, with which he illustrated his
lectures.   I am grateful to him for the
instruction I received ; although, if I yield-
ed to selfish feelings, I might fear that the

---

2 v. 4to. London, 1814, with 132 plates. They contain
the substance of many of the author's papers in the
Philosophical Transactions, but also much new matter,
particularly on the intestinal canal.

riches then displayed will render my poverty more conspicuous.

I cannot conclude this review, without noticing the labours of my friend Dr. Macartney; lately chosen professor of anatomy in Trinity College, Dublin, by the fellows of that college:—an appointment equally honourable to the givers and the receiver, having been bestowed on him, a perfect stranger, solely on the ground of his distinguished talents and acquirements. He pursued comparative anatomy with great ardour, and lectured on it for many years, at St. Bartholomew's Hospital. He is the author of a very interesting paper in the Philosophical Transactions,* on luminous animals, and of the articles CLASSIFICATION, BIRDS, FISHES, and MAM-

* 1810.

H 2

-MALIA, in Dr. Rees's Cyclopœdia; to which I can refer you for very excellent descriptions of the structure and functions of those classes.*

In the preceding short sketch I have endeavoured to point out to you the best sources of information on comparative anatomy, and, at the same time, by shewing you that men of the most powerful minds and great acquirements have found it an interesting as well as instructive field of inquiry, to excite you to follow their example. In enumerating their published

---

* That this gentleman may not lose credit by having the work of an inferior hand ascribed to him, I take the liberty of adding that the articles INSECTS, REPTILES, and VERMES, were furnished by myself at a very short notice, in consequence of Dr. Macartney, from whom they had been expected, being prevented from writing them by other occupations.

works, I do not wish that you should confine yourself to their perusal;—I rather exhort you to do as they have done, to study the book of nature, which you cannot resort to without receiving knowledge and gratification. At the same time, in a science which includes inquiries so various, and details so endless, you cannot know without reading what has been done already, and what remains to be effected. You cannot examine all parts for yourselves; and must therefore depend in many points on the reports of others. "The Man," says Dr. Johnson,* "whose genius qualifies him for great undertakings, must at least be content to learn from books the present state of human knowledge; that he may not ascribe to himself the invention of arts generally known; weary his at-

---

* Rambler.

tention with experiments, of which the event has been long registered ; and waste in attempts, which have already succeeded or miscarried, that time, which might have been spent with usefulness and honour upon new undertakings."

The present age will undoubtedly be regarded as the most brilliant era in the history of comparative anatomy. · The noble collection, both of living and dead animals at the Jardin des Plantes, the zeal and the scientific views of the able men to whom these treasures are entrusted, the valuable Museum that adorns this College, and the lectures which in all parts of Europe are now devoted to the extension and diffusion of comparative anatomy, convince us sufficiently that it has attained its proper rank in public estimation ; we may rest assured that the real value of the pursuit in reference to physiology, to the illustration of human structure, and to the advancement of zoology, a science inferior to none for the instruction it affords and the interest it inspires, will henceforth secure to it its due degree of attention and cultivation. *

* At no period has Comparative Anatomy been so zealously pursued in Germany as in the end of the last, and the beginning of the present century. Besides the respected names of Blumenbach, Soemmerring, Schneider, Kielmeyer, Rudolphi (Beyträge, Berlin, 1812), Albers (Beyträge zur Vergleichenden Anatomie; 4to. Bremen), Treviranus (Biologie, 5 t.) Reil, and Autenrieth, the following are some of those, who either have been, or still continue engaged in cultivating it, and who have communicated to the public the results of their inquiries.

Meckel (Beyträge zur vergleich. Anat. 2 t. Abhandlungen aus der menschlichen und vergleich. Anat.)

Wiedemann (Archiv fur Zoologie und Zootomie.)

In the lectures, which I shall have the honour of delivering to you, I shall attempt

---

Metzger (Opusc. Anat. et Physiol. Goth. 1790.)

Josephi (Anatomie der Saügethiere.)

Froriep (Bibliothek der Vergleich. Anat.)

Merrem (Vermischte Abhandlungen.)

Fischer (Ueber die Schwimmblase der Fische: üb. die Verschiedne form der intermaxillar-knochens: Anatomie der Maki: Naturhistorische Fragmente.)

Oken und Kieser (Beyträge zur Zoologie, Vergleich. Anat. und Physiologie; 1806 et seq.)

Posselt (Beyträge zur Anatomie der Insecten.)

Spix (Cephalogenesis, fol. l'Anatomie de l'actinia coriacea, et de l'astérie rouge in Annales du Mus. Nat. d'Hist. Nat. t. 13.)

Ebel (Obs. Neurolog. ex Anatome Comparata.)

J. et C. Wenzel (de Structura cerebri humani et brutorum, fol. Tubingen, 1812.

Rosenthal (de Organo Olfactus quorundum Animalium: Ichthyotomische tafeln, Berlin, 4to. 1812.

to exhibit a general view of the structure and functions of animals, describing each

---

Kieser (de Anamorphosi Oculi; Goett. 1814, 4to.)

Succow (Specimen Myologiæ insectorum; Heidelb. 4to. 1813.)

Nitsch (Osteographische Beyträge zur Naturgeschichte der Vögel; Lips. 1811, 8vo.)

Lorenz (de pelvi Reptilium; Hal. 1807, 8vo.)

Tiedemann (Anatomie des Fischherzens, Landshut, 1809, 4to.)

Tilesius (de respiratione sepiæ Officinalis; über die sogenannte Seemaüse, oder hornartige Fischeyer.)

Sorg (disquisitio physiologica circa Respirationem insectorum et vermium Rudolstadt, 1805, 8vo.)

Hausmann (Commentatio de Animalium exsanguium respiratione.   Hanov. 1803, 4to.)

Neergaard (Vergleichende Anatomie der Verdauungswerkzeuge.)

Ramdohr (Verdauungswerkzeuge der Insecten, Hal. 1811.)

part, so far at least as my own information,
and the means of illustration afforded by

Stosch (de omentis Mammalium, partibusque illis
similibus. Berol. 1807, 8vo.)

Jörg (über das Gebärorgan des Menschen, und der
Saügethiere, in Schwangern und nichtschwangern
Zustande, Leipz. 1808, fol.)·

Tannenberg (Mannliche Zeugungstheile der Vögel.
Gött. 1789, 4to.)

Tredern (ovi avium et Incubationis Historiæ pro-
dromus; Jena, 1808, 4to.)

Spangenberg (disquisitio circa partes genitales fæ-
mineas avium, Goett. 1813, 4to.)

Cavolini (von der Erzeugung der Fische und Krebse.
mit Zusätzen von Zimmermann. Berlin, 1792, 8vo.)

Bonn (Anatome Castoris Lugd. Bat. 1806.)

Breyer (Obs. Anat. circa fabricam ranæ Pipæ,
Berol, 1812, 4to.)

See also the collections published by the Natural
History Society of Berlin (Gesellschaft der Naturfor-

the Museum extend, in all classes of the
animal kingdom.   The plan of the course

---

schender Freunde), by the Academy of Münich (Denk-
schriften der Königl. Academie der Wissenschaften);
Voigts Magazin für das neueste aus der Physik, &c.
&c.

In Italy we may recite the names of Comparetti,
Poli, Malacarne (Encefalotomia di alcuni Quadrupedi,
1795.)

Mangili (de Systemate nerveo hirudinis, lumbrici
terrestris, aliorumque Vermium, 1795; Sopra alcune
Specie di Conchiglie bivalvi, 1804)

Penada (Osservazioni e Memorie Anatomiche; Sagg.
2. Padua, 1800, 4to.)

Moreschi (della Milza in tutti gli Animali Verte-
brali; Milan, 1803.)

Brugnone, Girardi, Rossi, &c. &c. whose contributions will be found in the Commentarii Instituti
Bononiensis; in the Atti di Sièna; the Memorie della
Societa Italiana; the Memoires de l'Acad. de Turin,
&c. &c.

therefore will be physiological; the order
depending on the arrangement, which may
be adopted, of the organs or functions.   In
natural history, where the object is to bring
us acquainted with each animal, with its
external form, its habits and structure, the
species are described separately : this plan
however is altogether unsuited to our present purpose, as it would be attended with
endless repetitions, and would exhibit the
facts in so detached and insulated a form,
that very little use could be made of them
for the purpose of general physiology.
What a confused medley of uninteresting
particulars would be found in lectures, in
which the animals should be taken in succession, and all the parts of each be described one after the other.   The analogies,
the comparisons, the gradual deviations
connected with changes of habit and circumstances, every thing in short, that in-
fuses life and interest into the subject,

would be lost.   The physiological plan has
the further advantage of being that on
which the Hunterian collection is arranged,
and which has been followed in the works
of Blumenbach and Cuvier.

I say that I shall *attempt* to follow each
organ through the whole series of living
beings.   That our knowledge of general
anatomy, even with all the accessions it
has derived from the labours of the zoologists already alluded to in this lecture, is
far from sufficient to allow such a plan to
be perfectly executed, in any organ, you
must be well aware.   Consider the multitude of animals, and the labour necessary
to know any one perfectly, and you will
be at no loss to account for the numerous
deficiences in any series of structures, that
can be submitted to your view.   Haller, a
most competent judge of such a subject,
declares that twenty years are not sufficient

for acquiring a perfect knowledge of human anatomy.   Now the species of animals, hitherto ascertained, in all the classes taken together, amount to many thousands.

Before however we begin to describe the structure of animals, their arrangement must be understood.   Comparative anatomy and natural history cannot be separated without great mutual injury.   It will be necessary for me to explain to you the principles on which the distribution of the animal kingdom has been regulated, and to detail to you the divisions now generally adopted.   The lectures would be unintelligible without this; as the names of. classes, orders, and genera will be perpetually occurring.   The use of these terms is a most convenient method of abridging our descriptions: the name of a class, order, or genus, saves us the trouble of enumerating specifically all the animals which it comprehends. The anatomical and physiological description will of course be preceded by a view of the classific arrangements of the animal kingdom : I think it will also be found advantageous, before entering on the latter subject, to give you a general notion of the structure and functions of animals, that you may form some `idea of the diversities, which the organs exhibit in the various classes.

I shall begin then by a sketch of the functions exercised by living bodies, and of the principal differences presented by their organs: this will be followed by a review of the animal kingdom according to the divisions generally adopted by naturalists; and I shall proceed, in the last place, to consider the particular organs and functions, tracing each through all the classes.

I have endeavoured to shew you that
the subject of these Lectures, as laying the
ground-work of general physiology, is es-
sentially interwoven with the very funda-
mental studies of our profession; and consequently that it has the strongest claim
on the attention of every liberal man, who
makes the healing art an object of scientific
investigation. The contemplation of nature, however, is not recommended to you
solely by its reference to intellectual objects; it exerts a beneficial and important
influence on the moral dispositions. The
tranquil occupation, which it supplies to
the mind, is a salutary contrast to the
restless agitation of avarice and ambition.
Its innocent pleasures are well calculated
to detach us from the frivolous and destructive pursuits of dissipation or de-
bauchery, and to lead us to estimate at
their true value the ordinary objects of

human exertion; on which we may then look down with the calm indifference so well pourtrayed by the philosophic poet:

Sed nil dulcius est, bene quam munita tenere
Edita doctrina sapientum templa serena;
Despicere unde queas alios, passimque videre
Errare, atque viam palantes quærere vitæ;
Certare ingenio, contendere nobilitate:
Noctes atque dies niti præstante labore
Ad summas emergere opes, rerumque potiri.
O miseras hominum mentes, O pectora cæca!

LECTURE II.

ON LIFE.

THE structure and functions of animals —their organization and life—are the subjects of two sciences; *anatomy* and *physiology*. Although the functions are the offspring of the structure—or the life is the result of the organization—and the two are consequently connected, as cause and effect, they might undoubtedly be treated distinctly. It would be quite possible to describe an animal body, to enumerate all its organs, to detail the size, figure, connexions, and various sensible properties

I 2

of each, without saying one word of the
living powers with which they are endowed, the uses to which they are subservient, or the sympathies and mutual
influences by which they are bound together for the great purposes of their
creation.   We might certainly describe the
heart, measure the size of its cavities, and
detail their various openings and commu-
nications, without once speaking of the
blood, or its course,---without mentioning
the contracting power of the organ, or the
order and succession of its movements.
But who would undertake the wearisome
task of such a dry and uninteresting detail? or what patience could sustain the
attention of the hearer? What would you
think of the person who should describe to
you a watch or a steam engine in this
way? who should exhibit to you all the
parts, and shew their position, without any
explanation of their uses, without any re-

ference to that nice adjustment, and mutual action, which render the one subservient to the important purpose of marking the division of time, and enable us, by the other, to execute the most stupendous monuments of human labour, or to produce the most striking results of human ingenuity? As I cannot for my own part discern what purpose of utility, much less what end of interest or amusement, could be answered by such a merely anatomical detail, and as the separation of the science of organization from that of life seems to me most violent and unnatural, I shall not disjoin anatomy and physiology.

Our object being to take a survey of structure, and of the functions which it executes, through the whole animal kingdom, I shall inquire first, what we are to understand by an animal, and what idea we are to attach to life.

On this and all other occasions I shall endeavour to convey to you clear notions of the subjects which I propose for your attention; I will therefore carefully explain to you the sense of the terms employed, and avoid all those which have an equivocal meaning.

I exhort you to be particularly on your guard against loose and indefinite expressions: they are the bane of all science; and have been remarkably injurious in the different departments of our own.

Equal caution is necessary in verifying facts; the authenticity of which should always undergo a close examination. They are the foundation of our physiological reasonings; if they are insecure, the whole structure erected on them is at every moment liable to fall. So long as we attend to these two points, the scrutiny of facts and the definition of terms, our progress, though slow, will be sure. On subjects not sufficiently examined, it is better to confess our ignorance, than to attempt to hide it by arbitrary assumption and vague language. We thus mark out objects for further investigation. Most of the physical sciences afford us excellent models for the method of proceeding. Unfortunately the various branches of medical science abound with examples of all abuses; of facts loosely admitted, of words vaguely employed, of reasonings most incorrect and inconclusive.

I shall not be anxious to attract your attention by novelty, nor by multitude of details; but shall rather attempt to exhibit the various parts of the subject in their natural connexion and order; to lead you to a correct mode of reasoning; and to

the best method of investigating and cultivating the science.

Organization means the peculiar composition, which distinguishes living bodies;
in this point of view they are contrasted
with inorganic, inert, or dead bodies.
Vital properties, such as sensibility and
irritability, are the means, by which organization is capable of executing its purposes; the vital properties of living bodies
correspond to the physical properties of
inorganic bodies; such as cohesion, elasticity, &c. Functions are the purposes,
which any organ or system of organs executes in the animal frame; there is of
course nothing corresponding to them in
inorganic matter. Life is the assemblage
of all the functions, and the general result
of their exercise. Thus organization, vital
properties, functions, and life are expres-

sions related to each other; in which organization is the instrument, vital properties the acting power, function the mode
of action, and life the result.

The matter that surrounds us is divided
into two great classes, living and dead;
the latter is governed by physical laws,
such as attraction, gravitation, chemical
affinity; and it exhibits physical properties, such as cohesion, elasticity, divisibility,
&c. Living matter also exhibits these
properties, and is subject in great measure
to physical laws. But living bodies are
endowed moreover with a set of properties
altogether different from these, and con-
trasting with them very remarkably. These
are the vital properties or forces, which
animate living matter, so long as it con-
tinues alive, are the source of the various
phenomena, which constitute the functions

of the living animal body, and distinguish its history from that of dead matter.

It is justly observed by Cuvier that the idea of life is one of those general and obscure notions, produced in us by observing a certain series of phenomena, possessing mutual relations, and succeeding each other in a constant order. We know not the nature of the link, that unites these phenomena, though we are sensible that a connexion must exist; and this conviction is sufficient to induce us to give it a name, which the vulgar regard as the sign of a particular principle, though in fact that name can only indicate the assemblage of the phenomena, which have occasioned its formation. Thus, as the bodies of animals appear to resist, during a certain time, the laws which govern inanimate bodies, and even to act on all around them in a man-

ner entirely contrary to those laws, we
employ the term life to designate what is
at least an apparent exception to general
laws. It is by determining exactly, in
what the exceptions consist, that we shall
fix the meaning of the term. For this purpose it is necessary to consider living
bodies in their various relations with the
rest of nature; and to contrast them carefully with inert substances; as it is only
from the result of such a comparison that
we can expect to derive a clear notion of
life,

In reviewing the characters of organized
bodies, this very name will lead us to consider, in the first place, the nature of their
composition, and the points in which it
differs from that of inorganic substances.
Organization then, by the meaning of the
term, denotes the possession of organs,
or instruments for accomplishing certain

purposes. The character of an inorganic substance is to be found in the properties of its integral particles ; the mass, which they may compose, whether solid, fluid, or gaseous, is unlimited ; but its extent, whether great or small, neither adds nor takes away any thing that can change the nature of the body ; that nature residing completely in each of the particles of which the whole is an aggregate. Thus a single grain of marble has the same characters as an entire mountain. A living body, on the contrary, derives its character from the whole mass, from the assemblage of all the parts. This character, which is more simple or complicated according to the place which the body occupies in the scale of being, is altogether different from that of its component particles. Even in so simple a creature as the polype, the individuality of the whole animal is quite different from that of its component atoms ;

but this difference is much more striking when we ascend in the scale, as for instance in a quadruped.

Inorganic bodies are for the most part homogeneous in their composition; but they may be heterogeneous. This depends on the accidental circumstances, under which the aggregation has taken place. All living bodies, however simple in their organization, are necessarily heterogeneous, or composed of dissimilar particles.

An inert substance may present a perfectly solid, fluid, or gaseous mass; but all bodies possessing life exhibit in their structure both solid and fluid parts. We find in no inert body that fibrous and cellular texture, nor that multiplicity of volatile elements which form the characters of organized bodies, whether in those that are alive, or in those that have lived.

The masses of dead matter have no form peculiar to the species; even where they are crystallized, the form of the mass is not constantly the same. Living bodies however have always a form characterizing the species to which they belong, and not capable of change without producing a new race.

The component atoms of an inert body are all independent of each other: whether the mass they form be a solid, liquid or gas, each particle exists by itself, and derives its character from the number, properties, and state of combination of its principles, borrowing or deriving nothing from the similar or dissimilar atoms which are near it. On the contrary, the particles which make up a living body are dependent on each other; they are all subject to the influence of a cause which animates them. This cause makes them all concur in the production of a common purpose, either in each organ, or in the individual: and its variations produce corresponding changes in the state of the particles or organs.

Hitherto I have considered organized bodies in respect to their composition, to what we may call their passive condition, or state of rest. But it is from a different order of phenomena that the most impressive notions of life will be derived. We must view them in activity; we must observe them, surrounded by chemical agents, yet preserved from chemical action; maintaining a composition apparently constant and identical, yet keeping up an incessant motion and change of their particles, in which the old materials are discharged and new ones converted into their own substance; producing new bodies, the seat of similar active powers with themselves, yet

terminating their own existence by the
very action of the principle that has so
long preserved them.

You well know what happens to the
body after death : its heat is lost, and it
soon reaches the temperature of the surrounding medium : the eyes become dim,
the lips and cheeks livid ; the hue of the
skin is altered : the fluids contained in the
vessels, or cavities, and the substances
lodged in the viscera of the body, penetrate
their receptacles, and tinge all the surrounding parts. The flesh soon turns green
or livid, diffuses ammoniacal effluvia or
noxious exhalations in the atmosphere, or
melts away into an offensive ichor. Such
are the effects produced by the chemical
action of the solids and fluids of the body
on each other, and by the affinities of the
surrounding agents air, moisture and heat
to both. Yet the animal solids and fluids,

and the visceral contents were in mutual
contact during life; and the body was
surrounded by the same external agents.
But the vital forces were superior to these
chemical affinities, and superseded their
action : the destructive power of these
agents was suspended by the preservative
power of life. So striking an operation
could not fail to attract observation; and
life has been even defined by Stahl and his
followers, from this exemplification of its
effects, that which prevents decomposition,
putredini contrarium; now, although this
is too limited a view of the subject, inasmuch as the phenomenon in question is
only one out of several included under our
notion of vitality, yet it belongs to the
very essence of it, as we could not con-
ceive life to last a moment if this power
were withdrawn.

The regulation of animal temperature is

K

a remarkable illustration of the operation of vital powers : it attracted the notice of Mr. Hunter, and was made by him the subject of numerous and highly interesting experiments*. You know how soon heat becomes equally diffused through all surrounding inert bodies, the temperature of any one, that is either higher or lower than those around it, being speedily reduced or exalted to a level with them. Animals however maintain a certain standard temperature under all circumstances. The human body has one and the same heat in the intense colds† of Siberia, Spitzbergen,

---

* Observations on the Animal Economy.

† Captain Cartwright experienced a cold of —25° on the coast of Labrador, (Journal of a Residence, &c.); and Latrobe — 30° on the same coast, (Philosophical Transactions, 1783.) The cold at Petersburg and Moscow, has been from — 30° to — 39°, (Com-

and Greenland, where mercury freezes in the open air; and in the parched atmos-

---

ment. Acad. Petrop.) Mr. Patrin suffered — 35° in Siberia, and quicksilver froze, (Journal de Physique, 1791, p. 88.) Mercury has frozen at Prince of Wales's Fort, Hudson's Bay, and Albany Fort, (Philos. Trans. 1783; Experiments for ascertaining the point of Mercurial Congelation, by T. Hutchins; and History of Mercurial Congelation, by Dr. Blagden.)

But the greatest natural cold which has been ascertained by thermometrical measurement, was that experienced by the elder Gmelin, in January 1735, at Jeniseik, in 58° north latitude. The mercury fell to — 126°, (Flora Sibirica; pref.) The sparrows and jays were killed. When Pallas was at Krasnaiarsk, in Siberia, situated in 56° north lat. the thermometer fell on the 7th of December, 1772, to — 80° : as the scale did not reach lower, the quicksilver receded into the bulb and froze. A large mass of pure quicksilver exposed in the open air was rendered completely solid, (Reisen durch Russland, 3ʳ th. p. 118). Our countrymen experienced a degree of cold apparently as severe, although it was not measured, on the Churchill

phere of equinoctial Africa or America,
where the thermometer has exceeded

River, in Hudson's Bay, (Philos. Trans. No. 465,
p. 157.) Brandy was frozen in the rooms where they
had fires.

Although it is doubtful whether we can rely im-
plicitly on the above statements, respecting the exact
degree of cold, because mercury about the time of
freezing, undergoes a remarkable reduction of bulk,
so as to make it sink through a space equivalent to
some hundreds of degrees, (Cavendish's Observations
on Mr. Hutchins's Experiments, Philos. Trans. 1783,
and Blagden's History of Mercurial Congelation, ibid.)
Yet the other effects of such a reduced temperature
are sufficient to illustrate the point in question.   The
Canadian savages and the Eskimos go to the chase in
such temperatures; and the inhabitants of the countries visited by Gmelin and Pallas cannot remain constantly in their houses during the winters.   Even
Europeans, accustomed to warmer climates, can undergo the cold already mentioned, and escape unhurt,
if they take exercise enough.   The Danish settlement
of Noogsack, in Greenland, is in 72° north lat. and
some Dutchmen wintered, in 1597, under Heemskerk,

120°*; in the heated rooms of experi-
menters, where it has stood at 260°; and

---

in 76° north lat. on Spitzbergen. Some of them
perished, but those who moved enough, and were in
sound health at first, withstood the dreadful cold,
which the polar bear, (ursus maritimus) apparently
born for these climes, seems to have been incapable of
supporting. For the journal expressly states, that as
soon as the sun sinks below the horizon, the cold becomes so intense, that the bears are no longer seen,
and the white fox (canis lagopus) alone braves the
weather. (Voyages de la Compagnie des Indes; pt. 1.)
Three Russians lived for six or seven years in 78° north
lat. (Dr. Aikin's account of attempts to winter in high
northern latitudes, in the Manchester Society's Memoirs, vol. i.) Cranz too particularly observes, that
the Greenlander will expose himself to the piercing
cold of his climate with uncovered head and neck, and
very slender clothing.

* The power of the human body to withstand ex-
treme cold will appear in a more remarkable light,
when we observe in a contrasted view what heat it is

in the stoves used for drying grain, where
it has been as high as 290°, and where a

---

capable of bearing. Boerhaave thought that a heat of
from 96° to 100° would be fatal to the human species.
Now much greater degrees of natural heat have been
observed. Even in Sicily, when the Sirocco blows,
the thermometer rises to 112°, according to Brydone,
(Voyage to Sicily and Malta.)   Dr. Chalmers observed
a heat of 115° in the shade in Carolina, (on the Weather
and Diseases of South Carolina.)   Humboldt experienced a heat from 110° to 115° in the Llanos or
deserts near the Orinoco, in South America, (Tableau
Physique des Regions Equatoriales.)   Adanson saw
the thermometer in the shade at 108½° at Senegal, in
17° north lat.   Probably the country to the west of the
great desert is still hotter, from the effect of the winds
which have blown over the whole tract of its burning
sands.   Bruce observed it at 114° in Sennaar, and
119° at Chendi ; Browne at 116°, (Travels in Syria
and Egypt.)   In the cabin of a vessel off the coast of
Africa, Adanson saw it at 133°, which is the greatest
heat observed in the shade, (Histoire Naturelle du
Senegal, p. 81.)

heat of 270° was borne for a quarter of an hour*.

---

* These curious facts were ascertained by accident. Messrs. Duhamel and Tillet being employed in 1760 and 1761, in researches concerning the destruction of grain by an insect, exposed it to the heat of an oven in order to destroy the animal. Being desirous of ascertaining the exact temperature, they introduced a thermometer, but found it lowered when withdrawn, before they could note the precise degree. A girl employed in attending the oven, observing the difficulty, offered to go in with the instrument and mark the point, to which the spirit should rise, with a pencil. At the end of a few minutes she did this, and it was found to be 100° Reaum. = 225° Fah. She staid ten minutes longer, when it had reached 130° R. = 292½° F. On coming out her countenance was red, but respiration was not hurried or laborious, and she did not appear on the whole more incommoded than persons are by the greatest summer heat.

These facts appeared so surprising, and so much at variance with the notions entertained by philosophers

In continuing our investigation we soon
find that the force, which binds together

---

on this subject, that the experiments were carefully
repeated; when it was satisfactorily ascertained, that
the girls accustomed to the service of the ovens, can
bear a heat of 115° R. $= 258\frac{3}{4}$° F. or 120° R. $= 270°$ F.
for fourteen or fifteen minutes; that they can stay ten
minutes at the height of 130° R. $= 292\frac{1}{2}$ F. and that
when it reaches 140 R. $= 315$ F. they cannot support
it more than five minutes.

It is to be regretted that a quicksilver thermometer
was not employed in these experiments, as it seems
that alcohol expands irregularly in the higher temperatures, so that perhaps the above numbers require some
diminution. It may be observed, however, that meat
and fruit were baking by the side of the girls who un-
derwent these experiments.

Tillet, Mémoire sur les Degrés Extraordinaires de
Chaleur auxquels les hommes et les Animaux sont
capables de resister; Acad. Royale des Sciences,
1764.

the particles of a living body, does not confine its operation to this passive result.

See also Duhamel de Monceau Supplément au traité de la Conservation des Grains.

On the same subject some very accurate and interesting experiments were made in England, in which it was found that persons could stay for some minutes in a room heated to 260° Fah.; in which the breath of the experimenter impelled on the bulb of the thermometer reduced it rapidly, and the heat of the internal parts as shewn by the thermometer under the tongue, and by the urine, did not exceed the natural standard of 98° or 100°,

Experiments and Observations in a heated room, by C. Blagden, M. D. Philos. Transact. 1775, pt. 1, art. 12.

And further Experiments, &c. ibid. pt. ii. art. 47.

Experiments in a heated room, by M. Dobson, M.D. ibid. art. 45,

We see at least that living bodies can act
on other matter ; that they can convert it
into their own substance, and thus augment
the number of their component particles.
We find this operation as constant as the
exertion of that force, by which they resist
decomposition.   For the absorption of
alimentary matter, its conversion into nu-
tritive fluid, and the subsequent transmis-
sion of that fluid to all parts of the body,
experience no interruption : and, in plants
at least, there seems to be a constant absorption from the external surface.

Since however living bodies cannot increase indefinitely, but are confined in each
case within certain limits, they must lose
on one side what they gain on the other.
Accordingly we find, besides the immense
loss by transpiration, that there are constant movements of the internal parts,
changes in their condition, and losses of

substance connected with these alterations; thus we arrive at a very different view from that which we took at first; instead of a constant union among the component particles, we see a continued change, so that the body cannot be called the same in any two successive instants. We see a kind of circulation established, in which the old and useless elements are thrown out, and their place is supplied by new materials. The latter are deposited in the interstices of the particles already existing; or, technically speaking, they grow by introsusception.

In all these points there is a strong contrast in inorganic bodies; they are exposed to the action of all surrounding media: instead of exhibiting a constant motion, they can only remain unchanged in a state of rest; for, when any motion of the particles is excited, the body loses its form

and consistence, if the agent be mechanical, its very nature, if it be chemical :
their increase in volume is unlimited, and
dependent on accidental circumstances ; it
is effected by juxtaposition, that is, by the
addition of new particles on the outside of
the old ones.

Having thus proceeded, as far as we
can, in ascertaining the nature of life by
the observation of its effects, we are naturally anxious to investigate its origin, to
see how it is produced, and to inquire how
it is communicated to the beings in which
we find it. We endeavour therefore to
observe living bodies in the moment of
their formation, to watch the time, when
matter may be supposed to receive the
stamp of life, and the inert mass to be
quickened. Hitherto, however, physiologists have not been able to catch nature in
the fact. Living bodies have never been

observed otherwise than completely formed, enjoying already that vital force and
producing those internal movements, the
first cause of which we are desirous of
knowing. However minute and feeble the
parts of an embryo may be, when we are
first capable of perceiving them, they then
enjoy a real life, and possess the germ of
all the phenomena, which that life may
afterwards develop. These observations,
extended to all the classes of living creatures, lead to this general fact, that there
are none, which have not heretofore formed
part of others similar to themselves, from
which they have been detached. All have
participated in the existence of other living
beings, before they exercised the functions
of life themselves. Thus we find that the
motion proper to living bodies, or in one
word, Life, has its origin in that of their
parents. From these parents they have
received the vital impulse; and hence it is

evident, that in the present state of things, life proceeds only from life; and there exists no other but that, which has been transmitted from one living body to another, by an uninterrupted succession.

Inorganic bodies and their masses grow up from the accidental union of particles, or combination of elements; that is, they are formed in obedience to chemical and physical laws, of which we do not notice the action.

Foiled in our attempts to ascend to the origin of organized beings, we seek to inform ourselves concerning the real nature of the powers, which animate them, by examining their composition, by investigating their texture, and the union of their elements. In them only can the vital impulse have its source and foundation. In this branch of the inquiry nothing has been neglected; all the animal organs have been most closely scrutinized, examined in their mass and in detail, and analized into their constituent textures; each of which has been exposed to every variety of anatomical, chemical, and microscopic research. The animal fluids have been subjected, in like manner, to all the inquiries that the advanced state of modern chemical science could suggest, or its zealous cultivators execute. The result of all these inquiries, I have no hesitation in affirming, to be, that no connexion has been established, in any one case, between the organic texture and its vital power; that there is nothing, either in the nature of the tissue, or in the combination of the elements, of any animal structure, that could enable us to determine beforehand what kind of living phenomena it will exhibit: and consequently that this, like all other branches of human knowledge, consists simply in an observation of the succession of events. Would the mere examination of muscular fibres, without any observation of their living action, have ever enabled you to determine that they possess the power of contraction? Would a comparison of the fibres of the deltoid, the heart and the diaphragm have shewn you that the former will contract in obedience to the will : that the second are uninfluenced by the will, and that the third act both spontaneously and voluntarily? Would any length of contemplation have led you to discover, that medullary substance is capable of sensation and of thought? Could you have known from the structure of the stomach that it digests, or from that of the liver that it secretes?

These, and all the other particulars we know about the nature of living properties and functions, are simply the result of observation : consequently our labours on

the organic economy must be confined to
its history.

Lastly, the destruction of living beings
is effected in a peculiar and characteristic
manner. The very nature of life is to produce, after a time, which varies in the
different species, a state of the organs in-
compatible with the continuance of their
functions; this mode of termination, by
death, is therefore one of the laws, to
which organized beings are subject.

To these considerations I might add
others, tending to establish still further the
difference between physical and vital laws,
and consequently between physical and
vital phenomena : but it is sufficient to
have proved, as I shall now recapitulate,
that inert solids are composed only of similar particles, which attract each other,
and never move except to separate : that

they are resolvable into a very small number of elementary substances: that they are formed by chance, as we term it, or by the combination of those substances, and the juxta-position of new particles: that they grow only by the juxta-position of new particles, the strata of which envelope the preceding mass: and that they are destroyed, only by some mechanical agent separating their particles, or some chemical agent, altering their combinations. While, on the contrary, organized bodies, made up of fibres and laminæ, having their interstices filled with fluids, and resolvable almost entirely into volatile products, are produced by a determinate function, that of generation; growing on bodies similar to themselves, from which they do not separate, until they are sufficiently developed to act by their own powers: that they exhibit a constant internal movement of composition and decomposition, assimilating to

their own substance foreign matters, which
they deposit between their own particles :
that they grow by an internal power, and
finally perish by that internal principle, or
by the effect of life itself, exhibiting, in
their natural destruction or death, a phenomenon as constant, as that of their first
production.

We may establish then, as the general
and common characteristics of all organized bodies, that they are produced by
.GENERATION, that they grow by NUTRI-
TION, and that they end by DEATH.
Such are the particular notions included
under the term LIFE, when we employ
that word in its widest acceptation. This
description applies to vegetables, as well
as animals. But if there are many living
beings that exhibit only the degree of life
just described, there are many others, in

whom the process is much more complicated; in whom there are numerous organs,
executing appropriate functions. Our idea
of life must therefore be modified according to what we have learned by observation
in each instance. Thus the life of a quadruped will be very different from that of
an insect or worm.

In the study of the physical sciences,
we observe the succession of events, ascertain their series and order, and refer the
phenomena ultimately to those general
properties or principles, of which the name
does not indicate any independent existence, but is to be regarded merely as the
generalized expression of the facts. Thus
the chemist traces all the mutual actions
between the component particles of bodies
to their elective attractions or chemical
affinities; the natural philosopher sees

every where the exertion of gravity, elasticity, &c. These words denote what we call the properties of matter, and what are said to be the causes of the phenomena in question. · Experience does not shew us in what the essential action of any of these causes whatever consists, nor *how* any of the effects are produced : for example (to take a most common occurrence) we know not how motion is produced in a body by impulse. Experience can only exhibit the order and rule of succession of the phenomena, which indicate the action of the cause. When one event is observed constantly to precede another, the first of these is called cause, and the latter effect ; and we believe that the preceding event has a power of producing that which succeeds ; although, in reality, we know only the fact of succession. Hence, in natural philosophy, we only know the general

causes by those laws which experience has
established in the succession of the phenomena. These general causes, which have
been called experimental, inasmuch as they
are only known through the medium of
experience, have been termed indifferently
principles, powers, forces, faculties.

In our examination of the phenomena
exhibited by living beings, we follow a
method analogous to that pursued in the
physical sciences. We trace the succession of events as far as observation and
experiment will enable us to pursue them,
and we refer them ultimately to a peculiar
order of properties or forces, called vital,
as their causes. These vital properties are
the causes of vital functions in the same
way as chemical affinity is the cause of the
combinations and decompositions exercised among the component particles of

bodies, or as attraction is the cause of the
motions that occur among the great masses
of matter.

Whatever we see in astronomy, hydrau-
lics, mechanics, &c. must be ultimately referred, through the concatenation of causes,
to gravity, elasticity, &c. In the same
way the vital properties are the main
spring at which we arrive, whatever phenomena we may be contemplating in respiration, digestion, secretion, and inflam-
mation.

Among the most remarkable of these
vital properties are sensibility and irritability—the power of perceiving or feeling,
and that of contracting. To such properties we refer, in our ultimate analysis of
the functions, as the mechanician does to
elasticity, when he is explaining the mo-

tions of a watch, or the astronomer' to gravitation, in accounting for the course of the heavenly bodies.

But are these the only vital properties? will they account for all the phenomena exhibited by organized beings? Probably not, probably the analysis is not yet complete, or at least the powers, which observation has led us to discover, are not yet sufficiently distinguished. Sensibility implies consciousness; it is equivalent to the power of feeling; there is not only the capability of receiving an impression, but the additional power of referring that impression to a common centre; and this sense of the word is so strongly fixed by universal consent and long use, that its application to the vital acts, which are not attended with consciousness, strikes us at once not only as improper, but as contradictory. We cannot however avoid recognising that an impression is made, in various cases, on the animal organs, when no perception takes places. The blood excites the heart to contract—it excites the capillaries of the glands to those motions, which produce secretion, and the capillaries of the various organs to those operations, which constitute nutrition, yet we have no word in physiology to denote the impressions made in these cases, unless we employ, with a late acute and most promising physiologist, whose premature death I cannot but regard as a very great loss to our science, sensibility; to which I have already stated my objections. Irritability again, more particularly as it has been consecrated by long custom to that species of motion, which is exhibited by the muscular fibres, is not well calculated to denote the invisible operations of capillary circulation, secretion, &c. which are known only by their effects.

If we cast a comparative glance along the series of living beings, we shall observe the vital properties, either the fewest, or the least active at the lower end of the scale, and gradually increasing in energy to the upper. Vegetables are traversed by fluids, which circulate in innumerable capillary tubes, which ascend and descend, and afford the materials of growth and of various secretions. All parts of the vegetable must be acted on by these fluids, and the vessels must react on them to produce the various effects, of vegetable circulation, of secretion, absorption and exhalation. Their vitality resembles that of the bones and some other parts in animals. In the commencement of the animal kingdom, as in the zoophytes, there is a digestive

cavity, alternately distended and emptied;
here then the vital processes are attended
with obvious motion. Hitherto organized
bodies are fitted for supporting a mere
existence: but, as we ascend, they begin
to exhibit relations to surrounding objects;
the senses and voluntary motion gradually
make their appearance in worms, insects,
and mollusca; the vital properties necessary to the exercise of these functions being
added to what they possessed before. As
we ascend through reptiles, fishes, birds,
and quadrupeds, the powers of sensation
and motion become much more energetic,
much more active, and the internal life is at
the same time more and more developed.
Finally, the cerebral functions, which
are much more numerous and diversified
in the higher orders of the mammalia, than
in any of the preceding divisions of the
animal kingdom, receive their last development in man; where they produce all

the phenomena of intellect, all those wonderful processes of thought, known under
the names of memory, reflexion, association, judgment, reasoning, imagination,
which so far transcend any analogous appearance in animals, that we almost feel a
repugnance to refer them to the same principle.

If therefore we were to follow strictly
the great series of living bodies through its
whole extent, we should see the vital properties gradually increased in number and
energy from the last of plants—the mosses
or the algæ—to the first of animals---
Man.

I have pointed out to you the numerous
and obvious differences between organized
and inert bodies in their composition, and
in the history of the phenomena which they
exhibit. The vital properties of the for-

mer present an equally strong contrast to the physical powers of the latter.

The vital properties, constantly variable in their intensity, often pass with the greatest rapidity from the lowest to the highest degree of energy, are successively exalted and weakened in the different organs, and assume, under the influence of the slightest causes, a thousand different modifications. Compare the muscular energy of the same individual, when fainting, with that which he can display in a fit of rage, or in a paroxysm of mania. The physical powers, on the contrary, constantly the same at all times, give rise to a series of phenomena always uniform. Contrast sensibility and attraction; the latter is always in proportion to the mass of the body, in which it is observed, while the former is constantly changing in the same organ, in the same mass of matter.

The invariable nature of the laws, which preside over physical phenomena, enables us to submit to calculation all the facts in those sciences; but the application of the mathematics to vital action can only lead to very general formulæ, both because the different data are uncertain quantities, and because we cannot be sure that we have taken them all into consideration. The resistance experiénced by a fluid in passing through a dead tube, the velocity of a projectile, the rate at which a body falls through the air, may be easily reduced to a fixed law; but to calculate the power of a muscle, the velocity of the blood, or the action of the stomach, is, to use the comparison of Bichat, like building on a moving sand an edifice, which is solid in itself, but which quickly falls from the insecurity of its foundation.

From the circumstances just explained,

the vital and physical phenomena derive, respectively, the characters of irregularity and uniformity. Inert fluids are known, when they have once been accurately analyzed; but one or even many examinations do not inform us of the nature of the living fluids. Chemical analysis gives us a kind of anatomy of them; but their physiology consists in a knowledge of the innumerable varieties they exhibit according to the condition of their respective organs, or of the system in general; and to the mutual influences, which connecting the organs to each other, produce most important modifications of their functions. The urine differs as it is voided after a meal or after sleep; that is, according to the state of the digestive organs, and of the blood: in winter and in summer, or in proportion to the greater or less activity of the cutaneous capillaries, the mere passage from a warm to a cold temperature alters its composition. It is not the same in the child, the adult, and the old man; in the male and in the female; in a quiet state of the mind, and in the agitation of the passions. Add to these differences the innumerable alterations produced by disease, and you will be immediately sensible that the mere analysis of common urine constitutes a very inconsiderable share of the physiological history of that fluid.

The science of organized bodies should therefore be treated in a manner entirely different from those, which have inorganic matter for their object. We should employ a different language, since words transposed from the physical sciences to the animal and vegetable economy, constantly recal to us ideas of an order altogether different from those which are suggested by the phenomena last mentioned. Although organized bodies are subjected in many respects to physical laws, their own peculiar phenomena present no analogy to those which are treated in chemistry, mechanics, and other physical sciences: the reference therefore to gravity, to attraction, to chemical affinity, to electricity or galvanism, can only serve to perpetuate false notions in physiology, and to draw us away from the proper point of view, in which the nature of living phenomena and the properties of living beings ought to be contemplated. We might just as rationally introduce the language of physiology into physical science; explain the facts of chemistry by irritability, or employ sensibility and sympathy to account for the phenomena of electricity and magnetism, or for the motions of the planetary system.

The application of physical science to

M

physiology was begun when the latter was in its infancy; when organization had been little studied, and its phenomena still less observed. The successful employment of the just method of philosophizing, exhibited in the stupendous discoveries of Newton, did not advance the science of life. On the contrary, dazzled by the brilliancy of his progress, physiologists were even led by it into the error of seeking every where in the animal economy for attraction and impulse, and of subjecting all the functions to mathematical calculations. To Haller principally we must ascribe the merit of placing physiology on its proper basis, as a peculiar and independent science, by his unwearied industry in dissection, and more particularly by his numerous researches, in living animals, on all the parts of their vital economy.

The same means were pursued by Mr.

Hunter to a much greater extent, and with
superior success. He did not attempt to
explain life by barren a priori specula-
tions, or by the illusory analogies of other
sciences ; but he sought to discover its
nature in the only way, which can possibly
lead to any useful and satisfactory result ;
that is, by a patient examination of the
fabric, and a close observation of the actions of living creatures. He surveyed the
whole system of organized beings, from
plants to man ; he developed their structure by numberless dissections, of which
the evidences are contained in the adjoining collection ; and he discovered their
functions by patient observation and well
contrived experiments, of which you have
the results recorded in his works. He thus
not only strengthened and secured the
foundations laid by Haller, but supplied
many deficiencies, rectified several incon-
sistencies, and gave to the whole structure

an unity of character and solidity, that
will ensure its duration.

Such is the path, difficult and tedious,
but the only one, by which we can arrive
at a knowledge of vitality: to frame an
hypothesis, or even many, is a much shorter
and easier business.   To represent that
Mr. Hunter is the first or the only inquirer,
who saw the subject in a right point of
view, and prosecuted it on the right principles, who contemplated physiology as a
distinct science, that must be cultivated by
itself, embracing a peculiar order of phenomena, not to be elucidated by electricity, attraction, or what not, would be an
act of injustice to many enlightened inquirers.   But his labours, more than those
of any one man, embraced so wide a field
of inquiry into the composition and vital
phenomena of animals, that we might deduce
from them a rational explanation of many of

the actions of living beings, and thus lay the foundation for a general theory of life, that would not disgrace the name of Hunter.

In the science of physiology we proceed on the observation of facts, of their order and connexion; we notice the analogies between them; and deduce the general laws, to which they are subject. We are thus led to admit the vital properties, already spoken of, as causes of the various phenomena; in the same way as attraction is recognised for the cause of various physical events. We do not profess to explain *how* the living forces in one case, or attraction in the other, exert their agency. But some are not content to stop at this point; they wish to draw aside the veil from nature, to display the very essence of the vital properties, and penetrate to their first causes; to shew, independently of the phenomena, what is life, and how irritability and sensibility execute those purposes, which so justly excite our admiration. They endeavour to give a physical explanation of the contraction of a muscle, and to teach us how a nerve feels. They suppose the structure of the body to contain an invisible matter or principle, by which it is put in motion. Such is the ινορμαν or impetum faciens of Hippocrates, the Archeus of Van Helmont, the Anima of Stahl, Materia Vitæ of Hunter, the calidum innatum, the vital principle, the subtle and mobile matter of others;—there are many names for it, as each successive speculator seems to have fancied that he should establish his own claim to the off-spring by baptizing it anew. Either of the names, and either of the explanations may be taken as a sample: they are all equally valuable, and equally illustrative.

Most of them indeed have long lain in cold obstruction amongst the rubbish of past ages; and the more modern ones are hastening after their predecessors to the vault of all the Capulets.

The object of explanation is to make a thing more intelligible. Explaining a phenomenon consists in shewing that the facts, which it presents, follow each other in an order analogous to that which is observed in the succession of other more familiar facts. In shewing that the motions of the heavenly bodies follow the same law as the descent of a heavy substance to the earth does, Newton explained the fact. The opinion under our review is not an explanation of that kind; unless indeed you find, what I am not sensible of, that you understand muscular contraction better by being told that an Archeus, or a subtle and mobile matter sets the fibres at work.

This pretended explanation, in short, is a reference, not to any thing that we understand better, than the object to be explained; but to something, that we do not understand at all—to something which cannot be received as a deduction of science, but must be accepted as an object of faith.

If animals want such an aid for executing their functions, how is it that vegetables proceed without the same assistance? They perform vital motions, and exhibit some of the most important functions: do they accomplish them without an Archeus or a vital principle? have they no subtle fluid of life?

If the properties of living matter are to be explained in this way, why should not we adopt the same plan with physical properties, and account for gravitation or chemical affinity by the supposition of appropriate subtle fluids? Why does the irritability of a muscle need such an explanation, if explanation it can be called, more than the elective attraction of a salt?

To make the matter more intelligible, this vital principle is compared to magnetism, to electricity, and to galvanism; or it is roundly stated to be oxygen. 'Tis like a camel, or like a whale, or like what you please. You have only to grant that the phenomena of the sciences just alluded to depend on extremely fine and invisible fluids, superadded to the matters in which they are exhibited; and to allow further that life and magnetic, galvanic and electric phenomena, correspond perfectly: the existence of a subtle matter of life will then be à very probable inference. On this illustration you will naturally remark, that the existence of the magnetic, electric, and galvanic fluids, which is offered as a proof of the existence of a vital fluid, is as much a matter of doubt, as that of the vital fluid itself. It is singular also that the vital principle should be like both magnetism and electricity, when these two are not like each other.

It would have been interesting to have had this illustration prosecuted a little further. We should have been pleased to learn whether the human body is more like a loadstone, a voltaic pile, or an electrical machine: whether the organs are to be regarded as Leyden jars, magnetic needles, or batteries.

The truth is, there is no resemblance, no analogy between electricity and life: the two orders of phenomena are completely distinct; they are incommensurable. Elec-

tiicity illustrates life no more than life illustrates electricity.   We might just as well
say that an electrical machine operates by
means of a vital fluid, as that the nerves
and muscles of an animal perform sensation and contraction by virtue of an electric
fluid.   By selecting one or two minor
points, to the neglect of all the important
features, a distant similarity may be made
out; and this is only in appearance.   In
the same way life might be shewn to be
like any thing else whatever, or any thing
else to be like life.

Identity or similarity of cause can only
be inferred from identity or resemblance
of effect.   Which electric operation is like
sensation, digestion, absorption, nutrition,
generation ? which vital phenomenon resembles the attraction of bodies dissimi-
larly electrified, or the repulsion of those
in similar states of electricity? what func-

tion resembles the ignition of metals, and the firing of gases; the decomposition of water, and the subversion of the strongest chemical affinities?

Another assertion, which has been employed to prove the existence of an independent living principle, superadded to the structure of animal bodies, is, that the various beings composing the animal kingdom, and differing from each other so remarkably as they do, nevertheless exhibit the same functions. This argument, which has been adduced on other occasions, and for other purposes, is completely ungrounded. The fact is just the reverse. Comparative anatomy affords the strongest and most numerous proofs of the dependance of function on structure. Every variation in the construction of an organ is accompanied with a corresponding modification of function; and whenever an organ ceases to exist altogether, its office also ceases. The stomach indeed is very different in a man, a cow, a fish, a worm, and each of these different stomachs digests—but it digests after its own manner. If any organ can execute any function, why may not the urinary bladder digest, or the lungs form urine; why should not one organ execute all purposes. Were it indeed otherwise, all the interest and all the utility of the science would be at an end. All our praises of the wise adaptation of structure to situation and habits, of the modification of organs according to their uses, presuppose the truth I have just asserted. If this were not so, what end would it answer to classify animals according to their structure? How would this lead us to a natural arrangement, in which the place occupied by the animal indicates its construction, economy, and way of life? However, to cut the matter

short by an example or two, is the vital
economy of an insect the same as that of
a fish? or does that of either resemble the
physiology of a quadruped? Do the very
different teeth, jaws, muscles, stomach,
and intestines of a cow and a lion perform
the same offices? The visible fabric of the
brain differs most widely in quadrupeds,
birds, fishes, insects: is there not an equal
difference in their intellectual phenomena,
appetites, and instincts?

It seems to me that this hypothesis or
fiction of a subtle invisible matter, ani-
mating the visible textures of animal
bodies, and directing their motions, is only
an example of that propensity in the human
mind, which has led men at all times to
account for those phenomena, of which the
causes are not obvious, by the mysterious
aid of higher and imaginary beings. Thus
in the earlier ages of the world, and in less

advanced states of civilization, all the ap-
pearances of nature, which the progress
of science enables us to explain by means
of natural causes, have been referred to
the immediate operation of the divinity

The storm was the work of Jupiter, who
is sculptured with the thunderbolt in one
hand, and grasping the lightning with the
other: Eolus produced the winds; Nep-
tune agitated the ocean; Vulcan and Pluto
shook the globe with volcanos and earth-
quakes. So far was this belief in invisible
agencies carried, that each grove and each
tree, each fountain and each river, was
regarded as the abode of its peculiar
deity;—the fawns, the dryads, the nymphs
of the elegant Grecian mythology; the
sprites, the elves, the fairies of more modern
credulity. Poetry, which speaks the language of the people, and appeals to their

common feelings, is full of illustrations of this observation. Personification is its most common figure; and, so strong is our disposition to clothe all surrounding objects with our own sentiments and passions, to animate the dead matter around us with human intellect and expression, that the boldest examples of this figure do not shock us. In his sublime description of a tempest, Virgil not only makes the monarch of Olympus " ride in the whirlwind and direct the storm," but brings him before our eyes in the very act of hurling the lightning, and casting down mountains with the bolt.

Ipse pater, media nimborum in nocte, corusca
Fulmina molitur dextra: quo maxuma motu
Terra tremit; fugere feræ, et mortalia corda
Per gentes humilis stravit pavor: ille flagranti
Aut Atho, aut Rhodopen, aut alta Cerania telo
Dejicit.

Thus we find at last that the philosopher with his archeus, his anima, or his subtle and mobile vital fluid, is about on a level, in respect to the mental process, by which he has arrived at it, with the

" Poor Indian, whose untutor'd mind,
Sees God in clouds, and hears him in the wind."

It may appear unnecessary to disturb those, who are inclined to indulge themselves in these harmless reveries. The belief in them, as in sorcery and witchcraft, is not grounded in reasoning, and therefore has nothing to fear from argument. I only oppose such hypotheses, when they are adduced with the array of philosophical deduction, because they involve suppositions without any ground in observation or experience, the only sources of our information on these subjects. I

repeat to you that the science of physiology, in its proper acceptation, is made up
of the facts, which we learn by observation
and experiment on living beings, or on
those which have lived; of the comparison
of these with each other; of the analogies
which such comparison may discover, and
the general laws to which it may lead.
So long as we proceed in this path, every
step is secure; when we endeavour to advance beyond its termination, we wander
without any guide or direction, and are
liable to be bewildered at every moment.
To say, that we can never arrive at the
first cause of the vital phenomena, would
be presumptuous; but it is most true, that
all the efforts to penetrate its nature have
been equally unsuccessful, from the commencement of the world to the present
time. Their complete failure in every instance has now led almost universally to

their abandonment, and may induce us to acquiesce on this point in the observations of Lucretius on a parallel subject;

Ignoratur enim quæ sit natura animai ;
Nata sit, an contra, nascentibus insinuetur,
Et simul intereat nobiscum morte dirempta,
An tenebras orci visat, vastasque lacunas.

THE END.

BARNARD AND FARLEY,
Skinner-Street, London.

Just published, Revised and Corrected, in large 8vo. 3d Edit.

A

𝔗𝔯𝔢𝔞𝔱𝔦𝔰𝔢 𝔬𝔫 ℜ𝔲𝔭𝔱𝔲𝔯𝔢𝔰,

CONTAINING

AN ANATOMICAL DESCRIPTION

OF

EACH SPECIES:

WITH

AN ACCOUNT OF ITS SYMPTOMS, PROGRESS, AND TREAT-MENT.

𝔍𝔩𝔩𝔲𝔰𝔱𝔯𝔞𝔱𝔢𝔡 𝔴𝔦𝔱𝔥 𝔓𝔩𝔞𝔱𝔢𝔰.

BY

WILLIAM LAWRENCE, F. R. S.

PROFESSOR OF ANATOMY AND SURGERY TO THE COLLEGE; ASSISTANT SURGEON TO ST
BARTHOLOMEW'S HOSPITAL; SURGEON TO BETHLEHEM AND BRIDEWELL HOSPITALS;
AND TO THE LONDON INFIRMARY FOR DISEASES OF THE EYE.

MEDICAL BOOKS,

PUBLISHED BY

J. CALLOW, MEDICAL BOOKSELLER,

No. 10,

CROWN COURT, PRINCES STREET, SOHO;

*Who either gives the full Value for Second-hand Medical
Books, or Exchanges them.*

ADAMS'S (Dr. Joseph) OBSERVATIONS on
MORBID POISONS, in Two Parts; Part I. containing Sy-
philis, Yaws, Sivvens, Elephantiasis, and the Anomala confounded with them; Part II. on Acute Contagions, particularly
the Variolus and Vaccine. Second Edition, illustrated with
four coloured Engravings, copious practical Remarks, and
further Commentaries on Mr. Hunter's Opinions. By JOSEPH
ADAMS, M.D. F.L.S. Physician to the Small Pox and
Inoculation Hospitals. In one large 4to. Boards, 1*l.* 5*s.*

BREE's PRACTICAL INQUIRY into DISOR-
DERED RESPIRATION, distinguishing the Species of
Convulsive Asthma, their Causes, and Indications of Cure:
by ROBERT BREE, M.D. F.R.S. Fellow of the Royal
College of Physicians;—the 5th Edition, with additional Prac-
tical Observations; in 8vo.

BADHAM'S (Dr. Charles) ESSAY on BRONCHI-
TIS, with a Supplement, containing Remarks on simple Pul-
monary Abscess, &c. &c. 12mo. Boards, 5*s.* 6*d.*

CLARK'S (John) OBSERVATIONS on the Dis-
eases which prevail in long Voyages to Hot Countries, particularly to the East Indies; and on the same Diseases as they
appear in Great Britain; 8vo. Bds. 7*s.* 6*d.* 1809.

CARMICHAEL'S (R.) ESSAY on the NATURE
of SCROFULA, with Evidence of its Origin from Disorders
of the Digestive Organs; illustrated by a number of Cases,
successfully treated, and interspersed with Observations on
the General Treatment of Children. 8vo. Boards, 5*s.*

A. CORN. CELSI de MEDICINA Libri Octo
quibus accedunt, Indices Capitum Autorum et Rerum ex
Recensio Leonardi Targæ. In 8vo. Boards, 12*s.*

CUTHBERTSON'S PRACTICAL TREATISE on Electricity and Galvanism. By JOHN CUTHBERTSON, Philosophical Instrument Maker, and Member of the Philosophical Societies of Holland and Utrecht; illustrated with nine Copper-plates, Boards, 10s. 6d.

CROWTHER'S PRACTICAL OBSERVATIONS on the DISEASE of the JOINTS, commonly called White Swelling; with some Remarks on Caries, Necrosis, and Scrophulous Abscesses; in which a new and successful Method of treating these Diseases is pointed out. Second Edition, with considerable Additions and Improvements, by BRYAN CROWTHER, Member of the Royal College of Surgeons in London, and Surgeon to Bridewell and Bethlem Hospitals. Illustrated with seven coloured Plates, 10s. 6d Boards.— Ditto, large paper, with proof impressions of the Plates, 16s.

COOPER'S PRACTICE of SURGERY.—The First Lines of the Practice of Surgery, being an Elementary Work for Students, and concise Book of Reference for Practitioners; with Copper-plates. A new Edition, corrected and enlarged, by SAMUEL COOPER, Member of the Royal College of Surgeons, and Fellow of the Medical Society in London, &c. 8vo. 15s.

COOPER'S DICTIONARY of Practical Surgery: collected from the best and most original Sources of Information, and illustrated by Critical Remarks; including Observations on the most important Remedies, Applications, Instruments, &c. a copious Pharmacopœia Chirurgica, and the Etymology and Meaning of the principal Terms. The whole forming a complete Compendium of Modern Surgical Knowledge, for the Use of Students, private Practitioners, and Naval and Military Surgeons; by SAMUEL COOPER, Member of the Royal College of Surgeons in London, in one very neat and closely printed 8vo. vol. 2d Edition, considerably enlarged, Boards, 1l. 1s.

COOPER'S (Samuel) TREATISE on the DISEASES of the JOINTS; being the Observations for which the Prize for 1806 was adjudged by the Royal College of Surgeons; 8vo. Boards, 5s.

COPELAND'S (Thos) OBSERVATIONS on the Principal Diseases of the Rectum and Anus: particularly Stricture of the Rectum, the Hæmorrhoidal Excrescence, and Fistula in Ano: 2d Edition, considerably enlarged, 8vo. Boards, 7s.

COOPER'S (Samuel) **CRITICAL REFLEC-TIONS** on several important Practical Points relative to the Cataract; 8vo. Boards, 5s.

COPELAND'S (Thos.) **OBSERVATIONS** on the Symptoms and Treatment of the Diseased Spine, more particularly relating to the Incipient Stages; with some Remarks on the consequent Palsy 8vo Plates, Boards. 6s.

DAVIS'S (Dr. J. B.) Scientific and Popular **VIEW** of the FEVER of WALCHEREN, and its Consequences, as they appeared in the British Troops returned from the late Expedition—with an Account of the Morbid Anatomy of the Body, and the Efficacy of Drastic Purges and Mercury in the Treatment of this Disease, 8vo. Boards, 7s.

DAUBENTON'S OBSERVATIONS on **INDI-GESTION;** in which is satisfactorily shewn the Efficacy of Ipecacuhana, in relieving this as well as its connected Train of Complaints peculiar to the Decline of Life; translated from the French, 4th Edition, with additional Notes and Observations, by Dr. BUCHAN, 12mo. Boards, 2s. 6d.

FORD'S OBSERVATIONS on the **DISEASE** of the HIP JOINT, to which is added, some Remarks on White Swellings of the Knee, the Caries of the Joint of the Wrist and other similar Complaints The whole illustrated by Cases and Engravings taken from the Diseased Part, by the late EDWARD FORD, Esq. F. S. A. the 2d Edition, revised carefully, with some additional Observations, by THOMAS COPELAND, Fellow of the College of Surgeons, and Assistant Surgeon to the Westminster General Dispensary. Illustrated with 8 Copper-plates, 8vo. boards, 12s. 1810.

FARR'S (Dr. Sam.) **ELEMENTS** of **MEDICAL JURISPRUDENCE,** or a succinct and compendious Description of such Tokens in the Human Body as are requisite to determine the Judgment of a Coroner, and Courts of Law, in Cases of Divorce, Rape, Murder, &c. To which is added, Directions for preserving the Public Health; 3d Edition, corrected, and various Notes added by a Physician, 12mo. Boards, 6s.

GEOGHEGAN'S COMMENTARY on the TREATMENT of RUPTURES, particularly in a State of Strangulation. By EDWARD GEOGHEGAN, Member of the College of Surgeons, and Honorary Member of the Royal Medical Society, Edinburgh; 8vo. Boards, 4s. 1810.—" This work will be found highly interesting, as it proposes important improvements in the Treatment."

HOWARD'S (John) PRACTICAL OBSERVA-TIONS on the NATURAL HISTORY and CURE of the VENEREAL DISEASE; 2d Edition, in 2 vols. 8vo. Plates, Boards, 14*s.*

HUNTER (Dr. William) on the Uncertainty of the Signs of Murder in the Case of Bastard Children, 8vo. 1*s.* 6*d.*

JOHNSON'S PRACTICAL ESSAY on CAN-CER; being the Substance of Observations, to which the Annual Prize for 1808, was adjudged by the Royal College of Surgeons, London. By CHRISTOPHER TURNER JOHNSON, Surgeon, of Exeter, Member of the Royal College of Surgeons, London, and of the Royal Medical Society of Edinburgh · 8vo. Boards, 5*s.* 6*d.* 1810.

MEDICAL OBSERVATIONS and INQUIRIES; by a Society of Physicians in London. Vol. 6, 12*s.* Boards.

POTT'S CHIRURGICAL WORKS; a new Edition with his last Corrections; to which are added, a short Account of the Life of the Author, a Method of curing the Hydrocele by Injection, and occasional Notes and Observations, by Sir JAMES EARLE, F. R. S. Surgeon Extraordinary to the King, &c. 3 vols. Boards, 15*s.*

RICHERAND'S PHYSIOLOGY.—Elements of Phisiology, by A. RICHERAND, Professor of the Faculty of Medicine, Paris, &c. &c. The 5th Edition, revised, corrected, and enlarged: translated from the French by G. J. M. De LYS, M. D. Member of the Royal College of Surgeons in London, 8vo. 12*s.*

UNDERWOOD'S (Dr. M.) TREATISE on the DISEASES of CHILDREN, with Directions for the Management of Infants from the Birth, and now precisely adapted to Professional Readers; 6th Edit. revised and enlarged, 3 vols. boards, 15*s.* 8vo.

CALLOW's MEDICAL SUBSCRIPTION LIBRARY.

CONDITIONS.

An Annual Subscriber to pay............£2　2　0
Half a Year...................... 1　5　0
Quarter of a Year .... 0 15　0
One Month .... 0　7　0

Annual Subscribers in Town or Country, paying Three Guineas per Annum, allowed an extra Number of Books.

Two Octavos allowed at one Time; one Folio or Quarto is reckoned equal to two Octavos.

Lightning Source UK Ltd.
Milton Keynes UK
UKOW02f1341090314

227800UK00011B/587/P